Michael Springle
(Sprinkle, Sprengle, Sprenkle)

in Pennsylvania

An evidence based reconstruction
of his
life and land

1724 - 1831

Donna Bingham Munger

Brydon Research

In Memory of

Ralph Raymond Sprinkle
1877 - 1939
GGG Grandson of Michael Sprinkle
(Simon, Joseph, Henry, Henry, Michael)

and

Frances Margaret Sprinkle Bingham
1905 - 1957
GGGG Granddaughter of Michael Sprinkle
and daughter of Ralph Raymond Sprinkle

Cover:
1818 Melish-Whiteside map of York County,
W. Manchester Township
showing location of Michael Springle's land
(Springles M.)
Pennsylvania State Archives

Copyright © 2012
by
Donna Bingham Munger

Brydon Research
Yelm, Washington

Other books by the author:

Pennsylvania Land Records. A History and Guide for Research
The Bingham Family in the United States. The Descendants of Thomas Bingham of Connecticut
Connecticut's Pennsylvania "Colony," 1754-1810: Susquehanna Company Proprietors, Settlers and Claimants,
Volume I, The *Proprietors*
Volume II, The *Settlers*
Volume III, The *Claimants*

All rights reserved

Library of Congress Control Number: 2012936136
ISBN-10: 0615612210
ISBN-13: 978-0615612218

Contents

Introduction

1. Michael Springle's Life along Conestoga Creek   1
    Origin and Arrival   1
    Conestoga Homestead and Taxes to Pay   5
    Rudy Miller's Death and a Tavern Too Close   16

2. Michael Springle's Life along Codorus Creek   23
    Youngblood - Blunston Tract   23
    Land Ownership Troubles   29
    Transportation, Taxes, and Another Tract   37
    Farm, Home, and Family Life   50
    An Unexpected Death   66

3. Michael Springle's Plantation Lands   79
    Springetsbury Manor Resurvey   79
    Blunston Tract Deeds of Release   85
    Margaret and Henry Everhart, and the 1746 Warrant Tract   87
    "Fair Hill"   91
    Peter Builds his Mills   95
    Michael, Jr. Sells   97
    War for Independence; A Son Moves West   97
    Peter, Jr. Takes Over   101
    "Fair Hill" Partitioned   103
    First Court Case: Penn's Lessee versus Klyne   107
    Second Court Case: Conn et al. versus Penn et al.   109
    Clear Title   112

4. Epilogue   115

    Acknowledgements   118

    Notes and Sources   119

    Index   127

Introduction

Occasionally, a topic becomes so imbued with misinformation that a revisitation is in order. So it is with Michael Springle. His life and land in Pennsylvania is due a revision and accurate history based upon existing evidence. From my vantage point as the final Chief of the Division of Land Records, Pennsylvania State Archives; as a twenty-five year resident of Michael Springle's home area in Pennsylvania; as an academic historian who has been combining history and genealogy since 1976; and as a direct descendant through Henry, Michael's youngest son, I charged myself with this task.

The following monograph is the result of research begun in the late 1970s in the Lancaster, York, and Adams County court houses, in the Pennsylvania State Archives, and in the Historical Society of Pennsylvania in Philadelphia. Since then there has been a sea change in the availability of original records. Now, it is possible to access many records through the Internet. Records not available electronically are quickly sent surface mail by cooperative archivists. One can work from almost any locale.

By expanding upon the few original land and personal records that contain his name, a history of Michael Springle's life and land develops. During his lifetime, Michael's surname was usually spelled "Springle" and was so well-recognized that seventy years after his death surveyors and map makers were still using that spelling as the 1818 map on the cover shows. Other spellings such as Sprengle, Sprinkle, and Sprenkle were used occasionally. Perhaps the most accurate spelling was Sprengel. The English form, Sprengle, occurs in the formal introduction to the Inventory of Michael's estate. Sprengel is an Old German term which designates a clerical administrative area. Thus, *The New Cassell's German Dictionary* gives the preferred meaning of Sprengel (with a capital S) as a diocese or bishopric and the second meaning as a sprinkling brush (for holy water). Although pronounced in German with a soft "g", most English speaking people used a hard "g" when they saw the word spelled, hence by the second or third generation family members spelled the name with a "k." To be faithful to the historical record, I have used the surname spelling for Michael as it appeared in each record.

During his lifetime in Pennsylvania, Michael Springle lived first on the east side of the Susquehanna River in the area of Chester County that became Lancaster County and then on the west side of the Susquehanna in the area of Lancaster County that became York County after his death. Land and probate records show Michael as an enterprising, prosperous Pennsylvania German farmer. Building historically upon those records places Michael within the events of his environment.

Michael Springle's life did not end with his death, but continued as long as his land remained in the family. Deeds and estate records of his heirs and of his heirs' heirs show Michael's influence in their lives. Building upon these records reveals how Michael's land became a model in a legal case that slowly wound its way to the Unites States Supreme Court.

Conestoga Creek
Photo courtesy waymarking.com

1 Michael Springle's Life along Conestoga Creek

Origin and Arrival

Pennsylvania had been a colony for a trifle over forty years when Michael Springle first appeared as a landholder. The year was 1724 and Michael was listed as a taxpayer on the assessment list for Conestoga Township, then Chester County. Michael's last name was spelled "Springle" on the list and continued to be spelled that way during his lifetime, although sometimes when written by others, it was spelled Sprengle, Sprinkle, Sprenkle, or even in bizarre ways such as Spingle, Stringle, Sprigll, and even Arringall.

When and from where Michael came is not documented. Several researchers, in print and online, have made a variety of unsubstantiated statements about Michael and his family. Others have slavishly copied and perpetuated these undocumented "facts." A few offer very creative and, on the surface, plausible pedigrees for Michael, but until the authors offer up some serious proof based upon primary records, it is best to consider these as simply good stories.

In the first forty years of Pennsylvania, First Purchasers and their Under Purchasers - Quakers and others from England and Ireland - had settled much of Philadelphia, Bucks, and Chester counties. To expand further north and west, William Penn and James Logan, his Secretary for Proprietary Affairs, encouraged German and Swiss religious dissidents as well as Welsh and Scots-Irish. These groups were offered large tracts of land to subdivide and sell to others if they would settle along the frontier. Before settlement was well under way, William Penn died (1718) and the business of selling land came almost to a standstill, limited to the income necessary to pay his mortgagees while the Court settled his will. Record-keeping fell into turmoil, but immigration did not cease. Consequently, thousands of new settlers from all European countries entered Pennsylvania as undocumented aliens. Some bought land from earlier warrantees, some turned to neighboring Maryland for warrants, and some simply squatted on land and waited. For fourteen years, 1718 - 1732, settlers took matters into their own hands. Finding those people in later records is not difficult, but pinpointing their arrival may be impossible.

During colonial times, each colony had its own immigration and naturalization laws. Pennsylvania required Swedes, Germans, Swiss, and all others who had not held land in the Dominions of Great Britain to become naturalized before they could sell or bequeath land they had bought. Eager to cement their legal status as citizens, the Germans of Germantown declared their allegiance to the King and fidelity to the Proprietor of Pennsylvania in 1691, but it was 1709 before the Assembly passed legislation naturalizing them. Concern over their sincerity to become hard working members of society and improve their estates had allowed the issue to drag on for eighteen years! A list of the Germans naturalized appears in the published Pennsylvania Archives *(PA (CR): 2: 493-94)*, but according to Marion Learned "is so inaccurately printed that many names are unintelligible to any but the expert...." *(Learned, 172, note 43)*

More serious thought about naturalization began with Lt. Governor William Keith in 1717. *(On William Keith see Graemepark.org/History/People)* His arrival in Pennsylvania coincided with the arrival of three ships carrying a total of 363 Palatines. Keith considered it a security risk to allow so many "foreigners, from Germany" to enter Pennsylvania without knowing the language and laws and to disperse immediately after landing. Upon his urging, the Provincial Council discussed the issue and then ordered masters of vessels to produce "an Account of the Number and character of their Passengers" and required all who had already landed to report to some Magistrate within one month to take an oath or give assurance of their affection to "his Majesty and his government." Compliance was minimal; only Captains of the three ships arriving in 1717 produced lists of the Palatines they had imported. *(PA (CR): 3: 29)* Further enforcement was lacking, but Germans continued to arrive in increasing numbers by way of England. Other Germans and Swiss arrived overland especially from the colonies of New York, Maryland, and North Carolina. They settled scattered throughout the three existing counties, Philadelphia, Bucks, and Chester as far north as the Lehigh Hills and as far west as the Susquehanna River.

Immediately after taking office in 1726, Patrick Gordon, the next Lt. Governor, addressed the German immigration issue anew. Using the arguments that the Palatines transported themselves "without any leave obtained from the Crown of Great Britain," and settled "themselves upon the Proprietors untaken up Lands without any application to the Proprietor or his Commissioners of property," Gordon persuaded the Provincial Council to re-institute the 1717 requirements, but with more teeth. Captains were to turn in a list containing passenger names, occupations, and places of origin and passengers were to take a new oath in presence of a magistrate declaring their allegiance to the Crown and fidelity to the Proprietary of Pennsylvania before being released to go on their way. *(PA (CR): 3: 282-83)* Strassburger and Hinke give a detailed and valid discussion of the resulting ship passenger lists in volume one of their *Pennsylvania German Pioneers*.

Germans who had entered Pennsylvania before 1727, such as Michael Springle, also needed to take the Oath of Allegiance to legally convey their land to their children or to others. As early as 1717 the Commissioners of Property had cautioned "Martin Kundigg, Hans Herr and Hans FFunk" and their group of Palatines that they were under a "Disadvantage... their being born aliens" when they requested land near Conestoga and Pequea Creeks "for their own Dwelling." The Commissioners had also informed Kundig, Herr,and Funk that a petition to the Assembly for naturalization might well be approved because years earlier Queen Anne had set the precedent by approving such a law. *(Minute Book H of the Commissioners of Property. PA (2): 19: 624; Warrant for 10,000 acres to Bundely et al. see Warrant Book, 1700-1715, Commissioners of Property to Company of Switzers: 229-30, or Original or Copied Survey B-23-216; Indexed in Chester Old Rights, page 7, number 146)*

Kundig, Herr, and Funk were members of a small, close-knit group of Swiss Mennonite families who had arrived in September, 1710 on the ship *Mary Hope*. *(Chalkley 65-66)* Being fully aware of the Commissioners of Property warning and advice, and having early on received permission to petition the Assembly for naturalization only to have the process stalled, the Pequea settlers opted for strength in numbers in 1728. By then, the Pequea -

Conestoga Creek area was well populated with Swiss and Germans and most of them had warranted or purchased and improved their property long enough to prove their seriousness

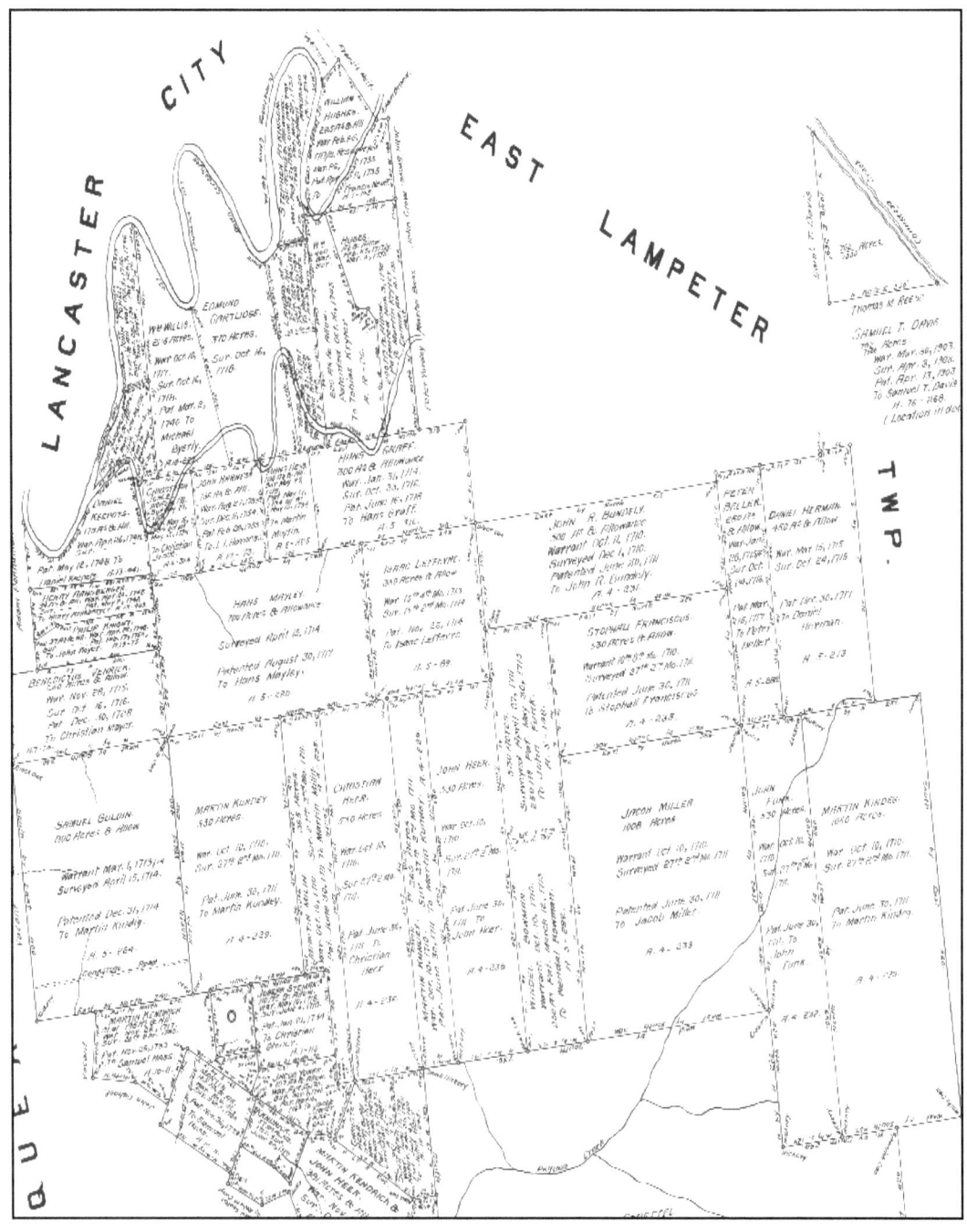

Martin Kindig/Kundigg tracts in the Pequea settlement
Warrantee Map, West Lampeter Township, Lancaster County, Pennsylvania
Pennsylvania State Archives

as hard working citizens. Meeting at Martin Meilen's/Meylin's house on 1 April 1728 two-hundred twenty-three Germans and Swiss signed either an oath or a declaration of allegiance and disavowal of any foreign power within the realm of Great Britain thereby qualifying them for naturalization. Some were Mennonites and others were not. *(Weir 1)*

By January 1729-30, Governor Gordon had investigated the case and decided that the petitioners had "generally so good a Character for Honesty & Industry as deserves the Esteem of this Government" and recommended passage of a bill for their naturalization. *(PA (CR): 3: 374-75)* Two different lists resulted from this process. As Weir et al. note in their article "German Qualification for Naturalization in Pennsylvania, 1728," not all petitioners who signed at Meilin's house were included in the act passed by the Assembly 14 February 1729-30. *(PA (8) 3: 1925-26); (Pennsylvania Session Laws (PSL) 4 St.L. 147 Ch. 309)* Partly this might be accounted for by an individual's failure to produce additional documents. If Rupp is correct in his *History of Lancaster County*, page 194, Germans and Swiss needed to submit a certificate of the value of their property from a Justice of the Peace and state the nature of their religious faith. *(For a chronological discussion of German and Swiss naturalization see Eshleman, Historic Background. passim)* From 1724, or before, Michael Springle was a neighbor of these petitioners, but his name was not among those who petitioned or were naturalized.

Conestoga Homestead and Taxes to Pay

After he arrived in Pennsylvania, Michael found a tract of land on the Conestoga Creek downstream from the Kendigs, Mylins, and Herrs. The tract had been warranted by Richard Carter, an Englishman who had moved in amongst the Germans. A resident of Chester County and a wheelwright, Carter had received a warrant for 200 acres of land between "Pacquean and Conestogoe Creeks near Susquehanah" from the Pennsylvania land office dated the 22nd day of the 6th month [August] 1716. *(Copied Survey D-77-144)* Entered in the Chester Old Rights Register page 10, under C, number 80, the clerk mistranslated the month as June. Carter agreed to pay twenty pounds within three months and the annual quitrent of one shilling sterling. The tract may have been surveyed on the 20th day of October 1716 as stated on the copied survey *(Copied Survey D-88-104)*, but we know that Carter did not pay the twenty pounds because the return of survey was dated 29 October 1739 and specifically states that payment in full was made in that year. Payment was required before a return was written. *(Returns of Survey (Loose), 29 October 1739)*

Carter lived in Conestoga Township for only a few years before moving east along Conestoga Creek where he found land more to his liking and squatted. He lived on that site long enough to be appointed a magistrate of the new township of Warwick when it was formed at the same time as Lancaster County in 1729. The town of Millport developed near

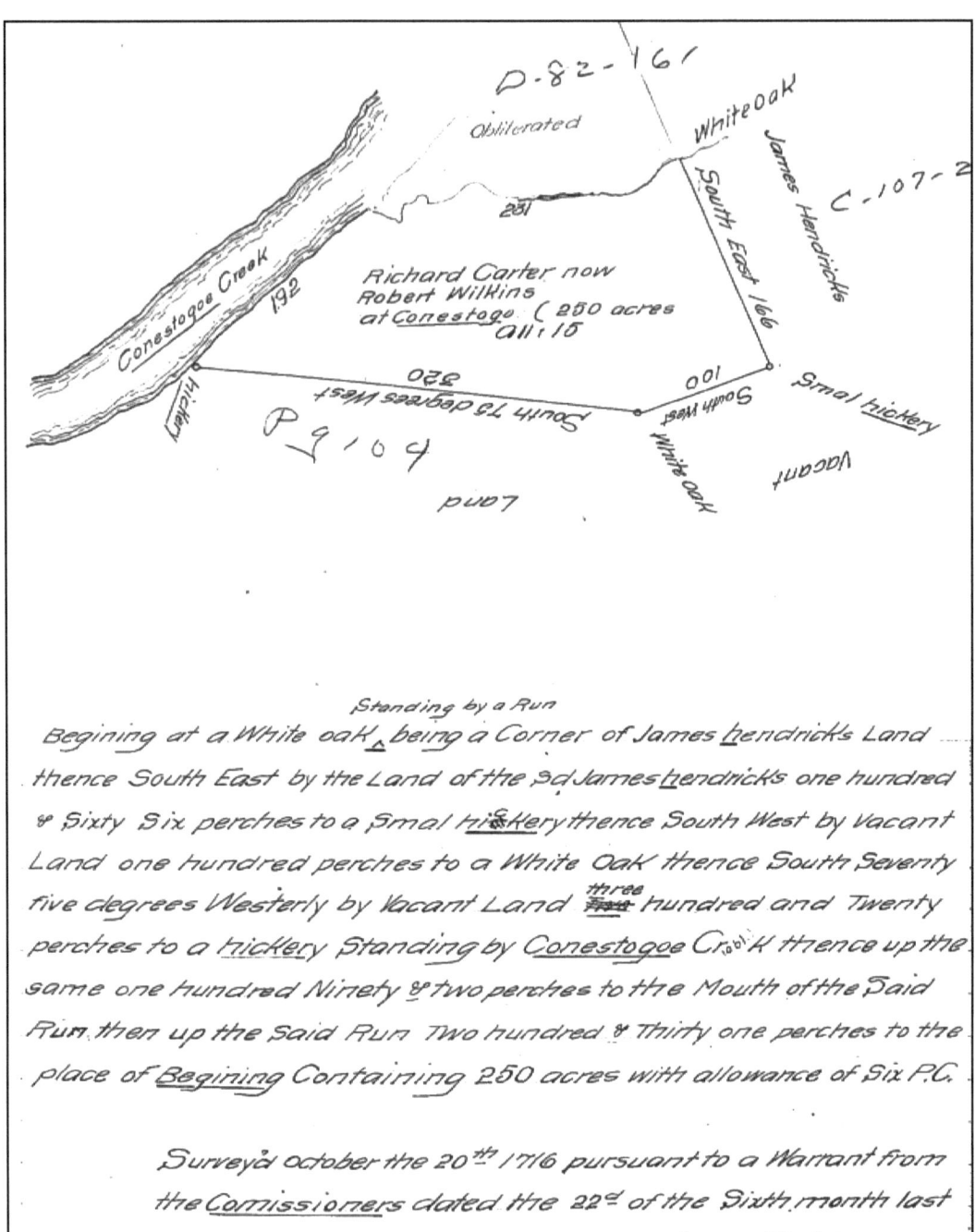

Richard Carter's Tract "sold" to Robert Wilkins, to Rudy Miller, assigned to Jacob Miller
Copied Survey D-88-102, Pennsylvania State Archives

Carter's place. A small spring named in his honor, Carter's Run, ran nearby. Carter died a bachelor in 1750 without having owned any of the land he occupied and was buried at the Union Meeting House, Warwick Township. *(Ellis and Evans 1072; Harris 132-3)*

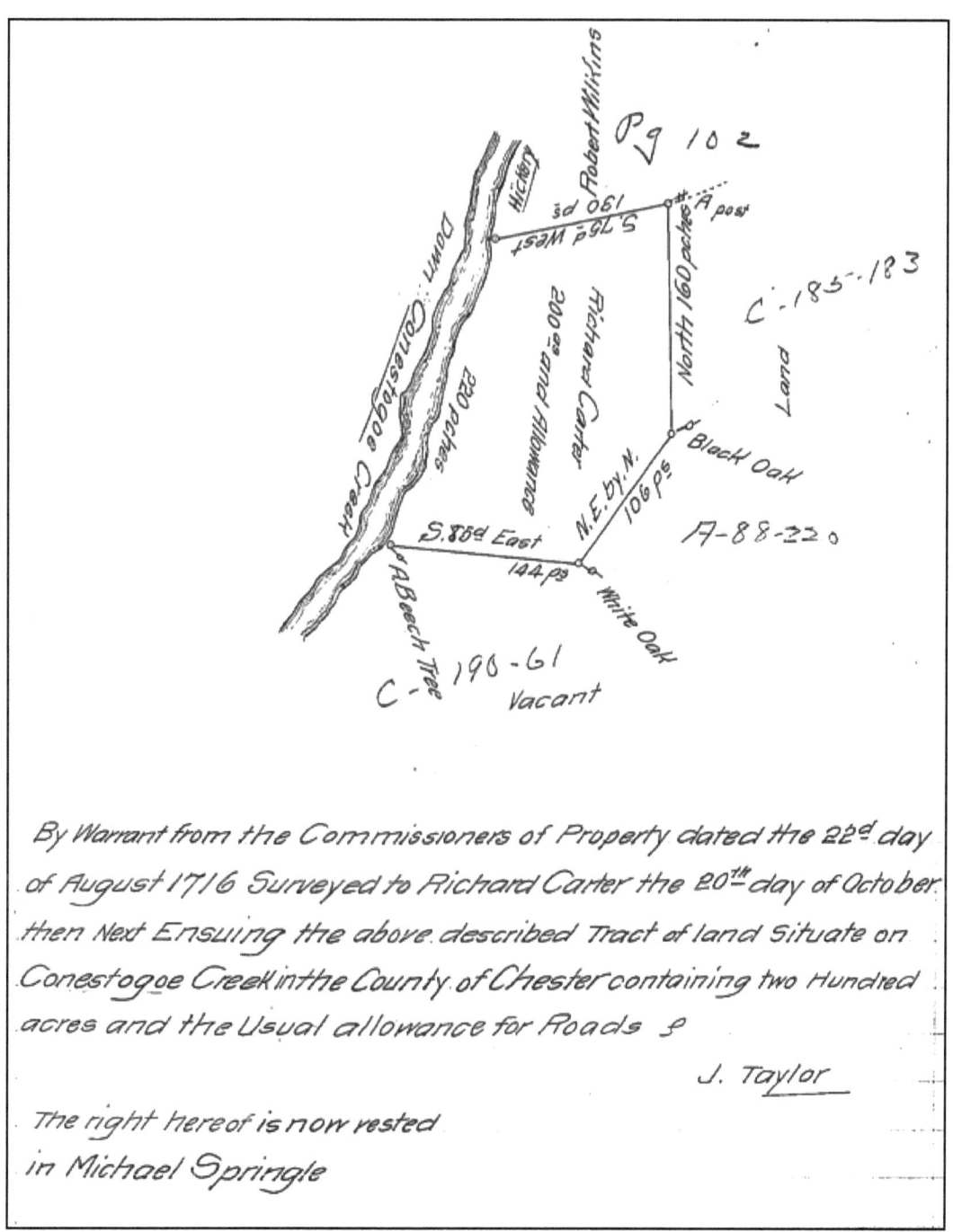

Richard Carter's tract sold to Michael Springle
Copied Survey D-88-104, Pennsylvania State Archives

Michael could have bought Carter's buildings or "improvements" on the 200 acre tract in Conestoga Township, but no recorded deed of sale exists as it would not since Carter had never completed the purchase. *(Chester County Deed Book Index 1688 - 1820)* We do know, however, that the 200 acres was located on the down stream side of a tract occupied by Rudy Miller.

Carter, also the warrant holder for Rudy Miller's tract, had obtained a second warrant for 250 acres dated 1 January 1717-18. Listed in Chester Old Rights page 10, under C, number 81, this time the warrant stated that Carter was "an inhabitant at Conestoga." *(see also Taylor Papers No. 2811 in Landis 10)* Clerk's preparing the copied survey books confused these two tracts and assigned the same survey date in 1716 to both, but this tract was surveyed at 250 acres. Carter "sold" this tract to Robert Wilkins, an Indian trader. *(Copied Surveys D-77-145; D-88-102)* Neither Carter nor Wilkins paid the Proprietary government for the survey, but Wilkins appeared on the Conestoga tax list for 1718. Wilkins undoubtedly sold the tract to Rudy Miller, a few years before Carter sold the 200 acre tract to Michael Springle. We are fairly certain of this because Ruliffe Miller's name appears for the first time on the Conestoga Tax List for the tax ordered in the fall of 1719 and assessed in January 1719-20 and Robert Wilkins' does not. Note that Robert Wilkins held a September, 1718 warrant *(Copied Survey D-69-267)*, for 150 acres in Conestoga which he entered and which could account for his name on the Conestoga Tax 1720-21, 1721 and West Conestoga 1722. He sold this tract to James Anderson, the Presbyterian Minister, in 1727 or 1728. *(Taylor Papers No. 3040 in Landis 13)*

A brief explanation of Pennsylvania's land procedures will help to understand the exchange of tracts. Pennsylvania was a proprietary colony meaning that William Penn, and later his three sons, John, Thomas, and Richard, were the sole owners of the land. They operated one land office located in Philadelphia. Everyone who wanted to buy vacant land needed to submit an application to that office. The application needed to state the amount of land desired and its location. Upon receiving the application, the land office wrote out a warrant or order to survey stating the location, number of acres to survey, and the price, and sent a copy of the warrant to the deputy surveyor in the particular area. Usually the applicant and the deputy surveyor worked together on the physical survey. Back at his desk, the deputy drew up a draft or map of the tract based on notes from his surveyor's book and sent the survey or draft to the land office. The land office filed the survey with the application and warrant until the applicant paid for the tract in full. If the applicant failed to pay, the survey remained filed until an assignee paid, thus making sure that only one warrant per tract existed. Whenever the applicant or an assignee paid the full price, the land office wrote an internal document called a return of survey. A patent, or final deed of transfer, soon followed. *(Munger 42-53)*

The juxtaposition of Rudy Miller's tract and Michael Springle's tract was no coincidence. Michael was married to Rudy Miller's daughter, Anna Margaret. When and where Michael and Anna Margaret married is not documented. Some researchers state that they married in Germany about 1720 before migrating to America, but that idea is beyond the realm of possibility. Rudy Miller was living in Conestoga Township in 1719 when the constable listed him using his full name, Ruliffe [sic. Rudliffe] Miller, as a resident to be assessed. The assessor valued his property at £32 which made him liable for a tax of 10s 8d to be paid to the tax collector in early 1720. His daughter, Anna Margaret, would not have been allowed to remain behind in Europe unless she had already been married. Another scenario would have Anna Margaret and Michael married before 1719 and living and migrating with her parents. Under that circumstance, the constable should have listed Ruliffe Miller with a son or son-in-law, but he did not. It is true that the appendage of "& Son" for Rudy Miller is inconsistent, but the assessment list of January 5-6, 1724-25 clears that matter up by listing in order, Mikell Springle, Rudall Miller & Son [Jacob], Henry Miller [Rudy's older son].

Detailed investigation of the hand written Conestoga assessment lists in the Chester County Archives gives further information about Michael's early activities in Pennsylvania. Called original records, these hand written tax lists were made from the assessor's working list or assessment book. As Lucy Simler explains in her Introduction: "To use the records it is necessary to understand the taxation process. The raising of a tax began with the issuing of warrants directing the township constable or assessor to draw up a list of the inhabitants ... and an account of their taxable wealth and to make his Return to the Commissioners by a given date. The Commissioners and County Assessors then met, rated, and assessed the inhabitants of each township. A list of the taxables of the township and the Rates they were to pay was prepared in duplicate, and one copy was sent to the township collector." Each person had a chance to appeal and a second set of rates was prepared in duplicate. Then the collector immediately collected the tax

As mentioned, Michael's name first appeared on the Conestoga Township assessment list for the year 1724-25, under the spelling *Mikell Springle*. The county commissioners had ordered the tax in the fall of 1724 when they issued their warrant to township constables directing them to make a list of inhabitants and their taxable wealth. Using the constable's list the commissioners assessed the tax on January 5-6, 1724-25, according to rates set by law. (Simler) Appeals were allowed during the next few weeks followed by a public notice of when and where the tax was to be paid to the collector. Since Michael was on the list, this is evidence that he was living on his tract in Conestoga Township in the fall of 1724 when the list was made. The surviving record, signed by David Jones Colector [sic], is a copy of the collector's list so dates from when the tax was collected, probably before March 25, 1724-25 using the Julian calendar, or March 25, 1725 using the Gregorian calendar. *(Chester County Tax Lists, Conestoga Township 1718-19 - 1726-27. Index online)*

The only other tax list that included Michael Springle was for the tax ordered in the fall of 1726 and assessed January 2-4, 1726-27. His name was entered as *Michael Sprigle*. Why his name is missing from the tax ordered in 1725 to be collected January 10-11, 1725-26 is unknown, but Richard Carter is listed. Perhaps the constable considered him to be the liable owner? However, that tax list differs from all other tax lists ordered between 1718 and 1726 in that someone alphabetized it in groups based on first letter of first name thereby destroying valuable clues and creating the possibility of error. The 1725-26 tax list is not an original.

Neither is Michael on any earlier tax list. The earliest tax list for Conestoga was ordered in 1718 and collected in 1719 after the appeal deadline of February 16, 1718-19. The county used similar procedures 1719-20, 1720-21, and 1721-22. In 1722, the colonial legislature passed a supplemental act "for the more effectual raising of county rates and levies. *(PSL 3 St.L. 295, Ch. 254)* The assessments were to be made by January 10, 1722-23. For that year, Conestoga Township was divided into West Conestoga and East Conestoga. Michael Sprinkle's name under any spelling was not on the 1722-23 assessment list. There is no extant tax list for 1723-24.

Replacing the 1722 law in 1725, the legislature set the tax rate at 3 pence on the pound. *(PSL 4 St.L. 10, Ch. 284)* On both the 1724-25 tax list and the 1726-27 tax list, Michael was a landholder. In January 1724-25 he paid 5 shillings tax and in January 1726-27 he paid 4 shillings 3 pence tax. Converting to pence, with 12 pence in a shilling, Michael paid 60 pence in 1724-25 and 51 pence in 1726-27. Dividing by 3 for the valuation, Michael's taxable assets were valued at 20 pounds in 1724-25 and 17 pounds in 1726-27.

Another observation concerning Michael Springle and these Conestoga and other township tax lists may help to clear up some earlier researchers inaccurate statements. Gilbert Cope, the noted Chester County historian, is credited for saving these tax lists from oblivion. According to H. Frank Eshleman, Cope resurrected the lists from the basement of the Chester County Court House in 1879 shortly before the County Commissioners were to sell them for waste paper. *(Eshleman, "Assessment Lists")* From these lists, Cope constructed his own lists that appeared under the title *"Lancaster County Tax List 1718 - 1726"* in the volume titled *Collections of the Genealogical Society of Pennsylvania Gilbert Cope Collection.* Cope's lists recorded tax payers alphabetically by last name, then grouped alphabetically by first letter of first name in chronological order instead of the original format of mixed entries in annual tax lists. For the tax date, he used - without explanation - the warrant date, that is, the date the county commissioners ordered the tax and not the assessment date. Neither did he include the valuations, but recorded only the tax assessed. Transcription errors also crop up. For instance, what is plainly written as "Ruliffe Miller" appears on Cope's list as "Rudall Miller." We might say, to be helpful, Cope destroyed a good portion of the value of the original tax lists. More important, Cope's errors have been perpetuated, unintentionally, first in Egle *Notes and Queries*, Second Series, page 131 and second by the LDS in microfilming his publication under the title "Tax List of Lancaster County, Pennsylvania 1718 - 1726." (FHL film 383296)

H. Frank Eshleman is also guilty of errors in his *"Assessment Lists ... of Lancaster County Prior to 1729"* a paper which he gave and published in 1916 in volume 20, number 7 of the *Papers Read Before The Lancaster County Historical Society,* available as an Internet resource at archive.org. After giving Cope credit for saving the lists, Eshleman explained that he had "copied these assessment lists complete." However, in copying, he missed the entry for "Mikell Springle" for the 1724-25 assessment. According to Eshleman's version, the name "Michael Springle" first appeared on the Conestoga Township tax lists for 1726-27. Eshleman had the assessment amount of 4s 3d correct, but he spelled the name "Springle" rather than as it appeared on the list as "Sprigle." This is a minor error; he probably changed the spelling on purpose because he had researched all the Conestoga Township proprietary land records for his "Map of Old 'Conestoga" and knew that Michael's surname was spelled Springle. *(Eshleman, "Old Conestoga Neighbors, 1715 - 1729." 271-293)*

Much more recently, two new indexes of the Conestoga Township tax lists 1718 - 1726 have been published. One, by my friends Gary T. Hawbaker and the late Clyde L. Groff, arranges the entries alphabetically which, as Gary says, "makes it a breeze to find an ancestor if he is listed." *(Hawbaker and Groff, v)* The other, by the Chester County Archives, is easy to use and alphabetical also. *(Tax Index 1715-1740)* Each index gives more than name and date, but for the historian, the alphabetical approach destroys other valuable information such as the original order in which the constable found residents - in other words - who lived next to whom. The original, hand written lists show Michael Springle and Rudy Miller and son listed one after the other corroborating the land records' evidence.

Exactly when Michael Springle took over Richard Carter's tract is impossible to determine. Carter remained on the Conestoga Township tax list as a landholder for the entire period 1717-18 through 1726-27 regardless of how long he lived there. My survey of the Rent Rolls does not show that Carter paid his quitent. Paying the quitrent was entirely voluntary. Newspapers announced when the Receiver General would be holding office in a particular county. It was up to the tax payer to pay in person. *(see for example The Pennsylvania Gazette, February 2, 1748. Accessible Archives)* Carter is not listed in the Rent Rolls as he would not be if he had paid nothing towards his warrant to survey. It is not likely that he paid anything towards his assessment, either. *(Rent Rolls no. 1-9, no. 10-12, 1703-1744. in Rent Rolls 1683-1776. Pennsylvania State Archives)* The reference we have to Michael's purchase of Carter's tract comes from a notation entered on the original survey. Dated 29 October 1739, the notation was more fully elaborated in the return prepared in the surveyor general's office. Stating first "R. Carter sold to Michael & William Springle," the notation continued "William re-

Conestoga Township Warrantee Map
Richard Carter's two tracts boarder Conestoga Creek on the east side
Rudy Miller lived on the northern tract; Michael Springle lived on the southern tract
Pennsylvania State Archives

leas'd his Right to Michael" and the right as of 29 October 1739 was vested in Michael Springle who sold to Joseph Stowman. Another note on the return stated that the tract had

Area Surrounding Conestoga Township Warrantee Map
Susquehanna River lower left; Conestoga Creek winding southwest from Lancaster
Springle and Miller tracts outlined in red
Google Map July 15, 2011

been paid in full in 1739 at £10 currency and one shilling sterling per 100 acres [quirent], the original price that Carter was to have paid. That note also stated that Stowman sold to his son, Joseph Stowman junr., and the tract was patented to him 14 October 1745. From

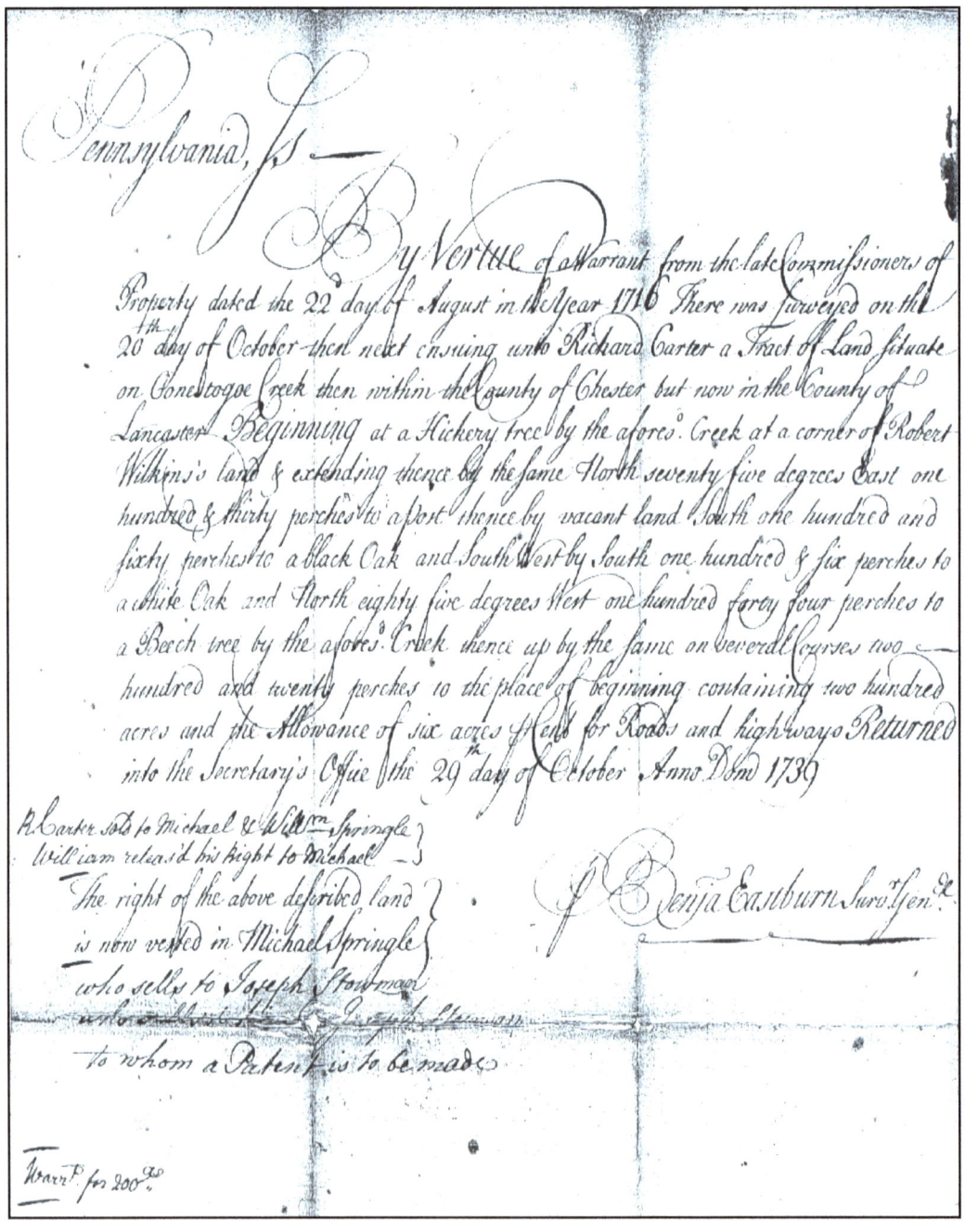

Return of Survey for Richard Carter's 200 acre tract on Conestoga Creek
Note that Carter sold to Michael and Willm Springle and William released his right to Michael Springle
Return of Survey, Loose, 29 October 1739; Patent Book A-12-391
Pennsylvania State Archives

the phrasing in the patent, it could be construed that Michael paid the £20 in 1739, but the patent clearly states that Stowman junior paid the additional five shillings due. *(Returns of Survey, Loose, 29 October 1739; Patent Book A-12-391)*

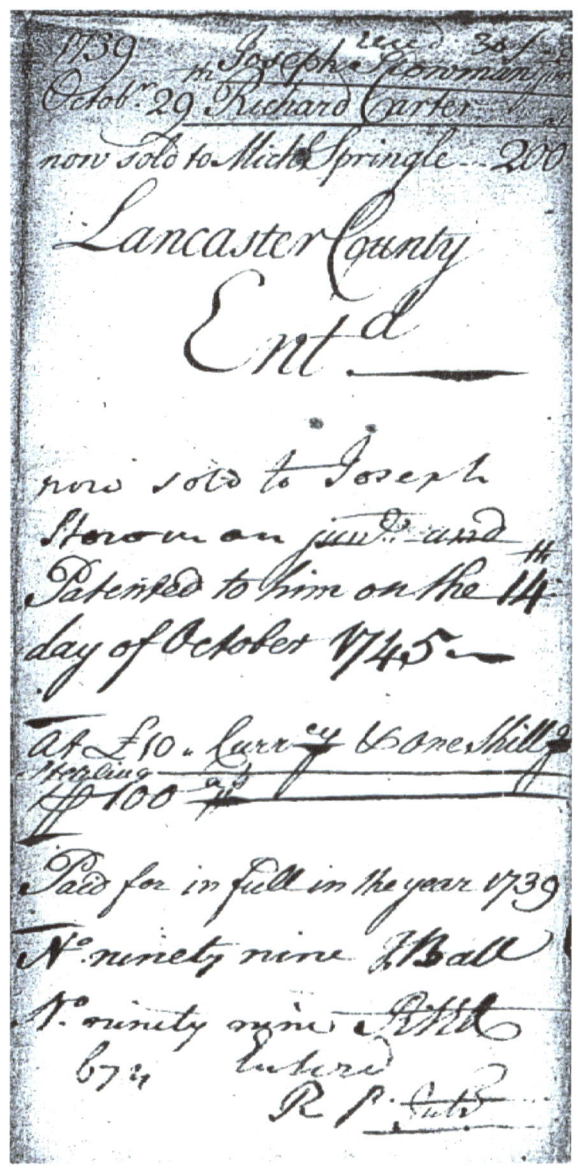

Reverse of Return of Survey for Richard Carter's 200 acre tract on Conestoga Creek
Notation shows that tract sold to Josephman Junr 1739, but patent dated 1745
Return of Survey, Loose, 29 October 1739, Patent Book A-12-391, Pennsylvania State Archives

Here is the only evidence we have that Michael Springle and William Springle may have been gifted, bought, or worked for, their first tract as co-owners, and/or that they were related. It may also be the earliest record naming William Springle. We might think that Michael and William Springle were brothers, but there is no documentary evidence of their relationship. Inference from this source might also make us think that Michael and William Springle lived in Conestoga Township until 1739. Our best source for corroborating these statements would be tax records, but tax records cease for Conestoga Township after the 1726-27 cycle. Furthermore, if William were under twenty-one in 1726 he would not have been listed as a freeman. Conestoga became part of Lancaster County in 1729 when that county was formed and from then until 1751 tax lists for Conestoga Township, Lancaster County do not exist. From other evidence, we know that Michael left Conestoga Township between 1727 and 1734, but no record of William Springle appears again until 1746 when he purchased a warrant for land near York Town straddling the Turnpike Road from York to Baltimore. *(28 October 1746, Lancaster County Warrant Register No. 507, Copied Survey B-1-5)* Although we have no evidence, it is possible that William lived on the Conestoga Township tract until then; or, it is possible that William moved to his York Township tract in 1739 and simply squatted until circumstances pressed his need for a warrant. Such was common practice. *(Hively, York 38)*

Rudy Miller's Death and a Tavern Too Close

Four years after Michael's name disappeared from the Conestoga tax lists, Anna Margaret's father, Rudy Miller, died. In Rudy Miller's 27 November 1731 Will, proved eighteen months later on February 21, 1732-33, he gave to his "Son in Law Mikell Springle Fifty Acres of Land to be run of my Plantation next joyning to the Land whear sd Mikell now Lives which together with what he hath formarly had is to be in full for my Daughter Ann's part of my Estate." *(Lancaster County, Pennsylvania, Register of Wills, FHL film 21354, Item 2, Book A, 9-10)* One interpretation of this bequeath could be that Rudy had bought Carter's improvement on the 200 acres for Michael and Anna Margaret and upon his own death was giving them both the 200 acres and the additional 50 acres.

From Rudy Miller's Will a researcher might think that he died a fairly well off yeoman farmer. His witnesses were neighbors Tobias Hendricks, John Postlethwaite, and Joshua Lowe, three of the most prominent men in Lancaster County. The record makes no comment that the Will was a translation from German, but the witnesses gave their solemn "Affirmation," not oath. The Inventory of his estate, return of survey, and patent records belie any assumption that Rudy was particularly well off. Instead, the Inventory makes the Will appear to be pro forma in that it contains statements that could never be met. In actuality, Michael and Ann received no land from Rudy Miller. Perhaps they had already moved to their tract on the west side of the Susquehanna River so gladly let Jacob have the fifty acres. Although Rudy Miller's Inventory did credit him with the 250 acres and buildings valued at £160, son Jacob ended up with the tract when the land office assigned him the patent for Richard Carter's 250 acres in 1748.

Rudy left wife Barbrey ten pounds Pennsylvania money, but not to be paid for six months after his death. She was also to get one half of the increase of his cattle and sheep

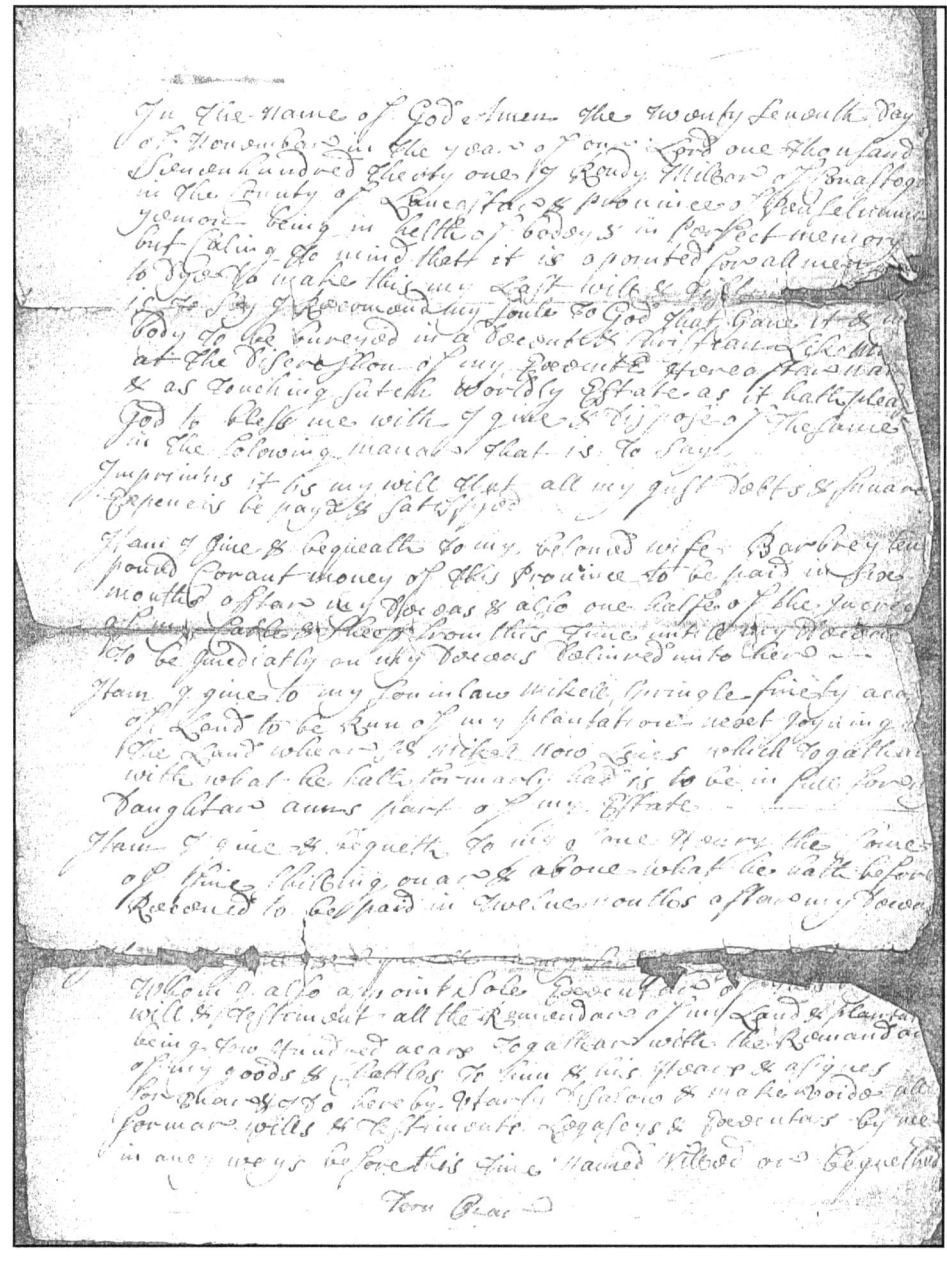

Roudy-Rudey Miller's Original Will, page 1
Lancaster County Archives

from the date of his Will, 27 November 1731, to his death, but his Inventory listed only one cow and one sheep. Rudy left son Henry five shillings besides what he had already given him, but not to be paid for twelve months. Apparently Henry was alive in 1731 and had not died in 1728 as some researchers have stated and others have copied. Rudy left son Jacob the remaining 200 acres of his land and his belongings. From the Inventory that would be the cow and the sheep, 20 flocks of bees, 8 pewter basons, a chest, 3 old table cloths, fine sheets all old, 1 stew [?] pan, 2 books, and his personal and wearing apparel. *(Estate Inventories, LancasterHistory.org)*

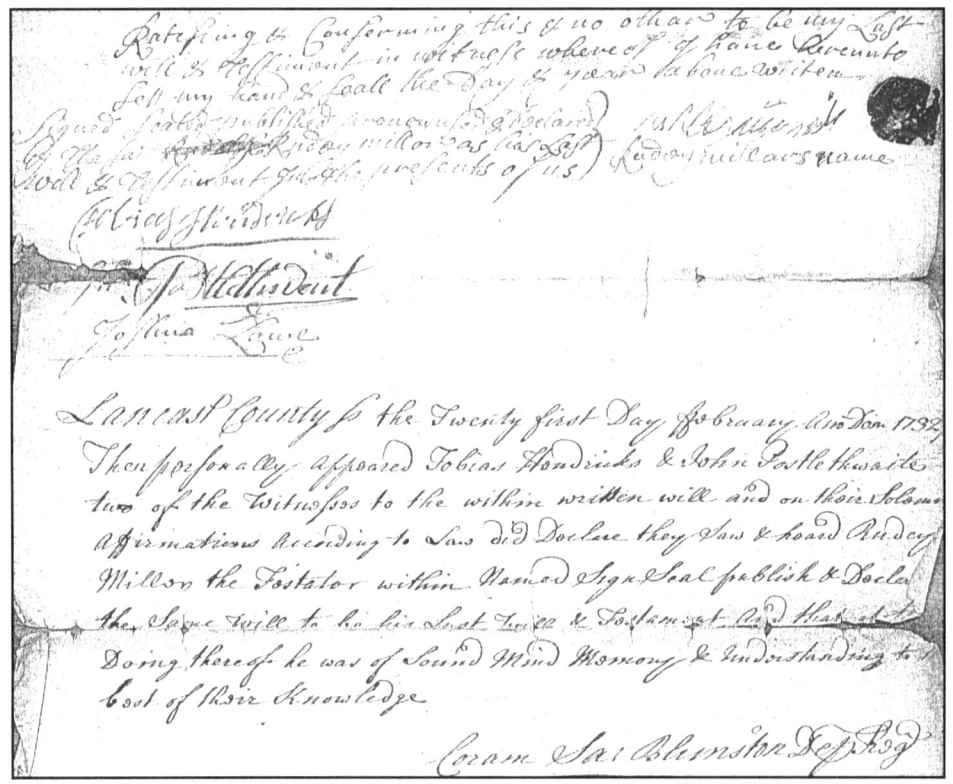

Roudy-Rudey Miller's Original Will, page 2
Lancaster County Archives

Where the 10 pounds for wife Barbrey was to come from is hard to say. Rudy's personal items and wearing apparel were valued at £23.12.34. They could have been sold. The value of the remainder of Rudy's goods totaled £13.15, the bees accounting for £6 of the total. It is doubtful that Jacob would have sold the bees since he would be continuing to farm.

Rudy Miller Estate Inventory
LancasterHistory.org

Michael and Anna Margaret Springle did not live long in Conestoga Township. All the good land had been taken up by 1726. At the most, they would have had only 250 acres to divide among their children, hardly enough to provide for a growing family. Furthermore, Conestoga Township was becoming quite populated. The 1726-27 rates showed 259 landowners and 22 non-landowner taxables in Conestoga Township and 389 taxables in the combined area of Conestoga, Donegal, and Pequea. *(Chester County Archives database calculation based on 1718 - 1727 tax lists.)* When Lancaster County was formed in 1729 it included more than seventeen townships on the east side of the Susquehanna River north and west of Chester County as it stands, today. No western limits were set; the assumption was that Lancaster County extended as far west as the Indian purchase treaties permitted.

By 1729, the county was no backwater community. Each warrant tract contained approximately 200 to 300 acres, but people lived only about two-thirds of a mile apart. For example, Michael's tract measured 220 perches along Conestoga Creek and Rudy Miller's tract measured 192 perches along the Creek. If each of their homes were in the middle of their tracts, the houses would have been about 200 perches apart. Converting, we get 3,300 feet and that equates to a little over six-tenths of a mile or one kilometer.

Even closer, on the road joining Rudy Miller's tract on the north, was James Hendricks' wayside tavern. A small creek ran between the two properties, as seen on both the warrant tract and Google maps. Where that creek entered Conestoga Creek the old trail from Philadelphia to Conestoga Indian Town crossed creating an ideal location for a rest stop. In 1729 Hendrick's niece Hylecha Hendricks, daughter of brother Tobias, Sr., and her husband, John Postlethwaite operated the tavern. Between June of that year when newly formed Lancaster County began business and August 1730 the County Court held sessions at Postlethwaite's Tavern. At the time, there were at least eight other wayside taverns between Gap on the east side of the new county and Logan's Ferry, now Bainbridge, on the Susquehanna River. *(Ellis 23, 202)*

Hendricks-Postlethwaite Tavern c. 1785
drawing by Johann David Schopf
Courtesy Conestoga Area Historical Society

Instead of choosing Postlethwaite's for the permanent Lancaster County seat, commissioner's selected a site further up Conestoga Creek and northward on a small stream. By the time the new Court House was ready for use in November 1730, the town had a population of about 200. *(Ellis 361)* Although most of the houses in the new town of Lancaster and surrounding townships were one story log structures, some stone houses did exist. Christian Herr had built a stone house on his tract in the Pequea settlement in 1719. Still standing in 2010, albeit restored, the house is a museum as well as the oldest existing building in Lancaster County. (Hans Herr House) Herr's neighbor, Martin Meylin, built his gun shop, also in 1719, of stone. Five years later, in 1724, he or his son, also Martin Meylin, applied for "about 100 acres in the Point in a fork of Conestoga Creek ... to make Tiles and Bricks."

(Minutes of the Board of Property, Minute Book I, PA (2): 19: 721 Mayley) Surely these were used for bake ovens, spring houses, and other farm buildings. About the same time, dating varies, Christian's brother Abraham Herr built a stone house for his large family. Located in Millersville, the Abraham Herr house, modified and restored, has a photo on the Internet. For Michael, Lancaster County was becoming crowded.

Christian Herr House before restoration
Courtesy Herr, Genealogical Record

Martin Meylin's Gun Shop
Photo Courtesy Wenger, et al.

Codorus Creek
Photo courtesy fellspointstudio.com
In association with Codorus Creek Watershed Association

2   Michael Springle's Life along Codorus Creek

Youngblood - Blunston Tract

The west side of the Susquehanna River held more appeal for Michael and Anna Margaret Springle so there they moved. By piecing together several records and reports, we can narrow the time to within a few years. Seemingly, they still lived in Conestoga Township in November 1731 when Anna Margaret's father willed them the 50 acres of his plantation next to their own 200 acres or he would not have done so. By April 6, 1734, however, they were living on the west side of the Susquehanna River "On the west Branch of Codorus Creek about two miles above the Fork," "upon an improvement" Michael "purchased of Peter Youngblood." This piece of information comes from Michael's Blunston License, so named for Samuel Blunston, a trained surveyor and deputy register for Lancaster County. Blunston functioned as the frontier monitor for Thomas Penn, then Proprietor of Pennsylvania and corresponded frequently with Penn and the Provincial Council of Pennsylvania, especially about encroachment issues with settlers from Maryland. Knowing also that the Five Nations would soon release their claim to the lower west side of the Susquehanna River, Thomas Penn had given Samuel Blunston permission in 1734 to write licenses to settle, especially to Germans who had already moved west and might be inclined to support Maryland claims if Pennsylvania failed to support them. *(Thomas Penn Papers (TPP): Thomas Penn to Samuel Blunston, August 8, 1734, 4:108-100)* These licenses were substitutes for warrants to survey and eventually would be honored when the area was opened for legal settlement in 1736. The thirty-second licensee, Michael's license was for 500 acres.

		acres	
30th Survey returned	Saml Chambers	200	To be taken where the same may be found vacant & Return the Bounds (N.B. no Bounds Returned)
30th No survey returned	Robert Chambers	200	To be taken where the same may be found vacant & Return the Bounds. (N.B. Returned that the same is taken Joyning on the river at a place called Rockrun Between John Harriss & Robert Millikins tracts opposite to a little Island)
30th Z.B. 200	John Mccormac	200	On the North side of Conedogwoint Creek on the Back side of James Corthys tract Bounded to the East by Saml Fisher tract.
April 6th No survey returned	Michael Springle	500	On the west Branch of Codorus Creek about two miles above the fork upon an improvemt. He purchased of Peter Youngblood.

Record of Michael Springle's Blunston License
Blunston Licenses, Pennsylvania State Archives

At the time, the 500 acres lay well to the west and outside of a 75,520 acre proprietary tract named Springetsbury Manor. That manor had been ordered and surveyed in June, 1722. Its southern boundary was to begin on the west side of the Susquehanna River opposite the mouth of Conestoga Creek and run west south west ten miles, then turn northwest by north twelve miles, then east north east to the upper corner of Governor Keith's 2000 acre tract called Newberry. The eastern boundary was the Susquehanna River. *(Bair, "Early Developments and Surveys West of Susquehanna River...." Annual Report: A 86-88; Original Loose Survey D-*

113-125) By convention, only the proprietor could authorize settlement within a manor as manors were intended to be the private property of the Penn family, the land to be rented, only, and the income going directly to the family. Blunston Licenses were to be written only for land outside of Springetsbury Manor, but by October 1736 nearly fifty German families were settled within the manor when Thomas Penn signed additional licenses confirming their tracts also, before opening the land office to settlement on the west side of the Susquehanna. *(Blunston Licenses 30-34; Munger 68-71)*

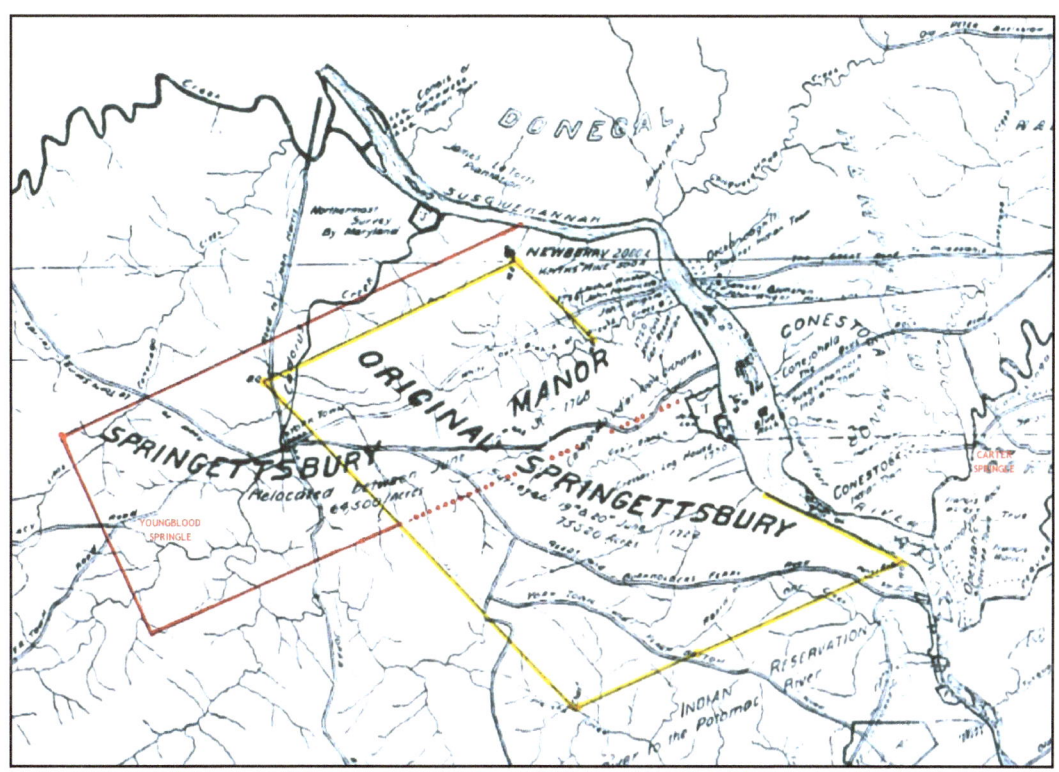

Springetsbury Manor Surveys of 1722 and 1768
Michael Springle's Carter and Youngblood tracts noted in red
Bair, "Early Surveys West of Susquehanna River" insert A68-69

More to the question at the time, did Michael's tract lay within Digges' Choice? Under an October 14, 1727 warrant, Maryland granted John Digges of Prince Georges County, the right to survey 10,000 acres in the backwoods. The survey began where Gresses's Branch intersected Conewago Creek and ran north placing the tract about four miles into Pennsylvania. Surveyors ran three sides, only, in April 1732 leaving one end open and giving Digges 6,822 acres. A Maryland patent followed in October, 1735. As settlers moved west, Digges subdivided and sold tracts to them developing quite a reputation for his efforts to attract Pennsylvanians to settle under his Maryland warrant. So much so that Digges' activities were grandly exaggerated in a 1731 letter from John Wright to James Logan. *(Wentz 70-71)*

To complete or to augment his 10,000 acres, John Digges applied to Pennsylvania for a warrant to survey land surrounding his Maryland patent. That failing, Digges applied for a Maryland warrant of resurvey for the missing acres and in October 1745 received a new patent for 3,679 additional contiguous acres that included several tracts already warranted and patented to others under Pennsylvania. Confusion and disturbances ensued, the Governor of Maryland mounted an investigation in 1746, the Justices of Baltimore County took depositions. One of those testifying, Robert Owings, deputy surveyor, age 47, claimed that he had laid out several parcels of land on the "little Conowago" [sic] within Digges Choice, as he remembered, between 1731 and 1734 and one of those tracts was for Peter Youngblood. Undoubtedly this was the same Peter Youngblood whose improvement Michael had bought. *(Deposition of Robert Owings. PA (1): 1: 695-96)*

Attesting to the confusion that existed, if Owings truly laid out his tract for Peter Youngblood on Little Conewago Creek, rather than on Conewago Creek, it would have been pushing the open end of Digges Choice far to the northeast. Digges Choice ran north from the South Branch of Conewago Creek and encompassed land where the city of Hanover developed. The Little Conewago runs parallel to Codorus Creek about two miles to the north of where the tract that Michael bought from Youngblood was located and more than twelve to fifteen miles northeast of Digges' Choice. *(For a complete study of each tract within Digges' Choice see Bankert)*

How did Michael learn about Peter Youngblood's tract? Possibly, through the Hendricks brothers. Their father, James Hendricks's 1,100 acre tract surveyed October 19, 1716, lay adjacent to the east of Michael's father-in-law, Rudy Miller in Conestoga Township. *(Copied Survey D-82-161; Conestoga Township Warrantee Map)* Between the Hendricks and Miller tracts ran the Conestoga Road and the ford through Conestoga Creek an ideal place for Hendricks's tavern. Hendricks's sons preferred to live closer to the Indians with whom they traded. Son John, wife Rebecca, and son James, Jr., settled on the west side of the Susquehanna River in the summer of 1728, where the main trail from Philadelphia crossed the Susquehanna. John Hendricks had applied to James Logan, provincial secretary, a year earlier, in 1727, for permission to settle on the west side. After learning that Marylanders were about to survey tracts in the same area, Logan had agreed and ordered Samuel Blunston to survey 1,200 acres for the Hendricks brothers "lying on the West Side of Susquehannah opposite to Hempfield ...." Finding the weeds so tall he could not chain a survey, Blunston marked only the corners of approximately a 1,000 acre tract. Faced with objections from the Indians who still owned the area, the Hendricks held off for another year waiting for Indian attitudes to change before they moved across the river. Blunston finally completed a partial survey of the tract in November, 1729. Three and a half years later, March 20, 1732-33, Thomas Penn signed an official proprietary warrant for the Hendricks survey and settlement. *(Original Surveys, D-113-181)* Located within the original 1722 survey of

Springetsbury Manor, the Hendricks' tract lay just south of Governor Keith's Mine Land also called Newberry. The brothers, along with Joshua Minshall, moved freely about the west side trading with Indians and meeting settlers from Maryland. *(Bair, "Biography of the Men Active in Early Developments and Surveys West of Susquehanna River 65)*

> Whereas upon the application of John & James Hendricks & some others, Inhabitants of Pensilvania, the Comissioners of Property did in the Year 1728 order Samuel Blunston to lay out a Tract of Land of Twelve hundred Acres lying on the West Side of Susquehannah opposite to Hempfield; which Land was then sur[veyed?] the said Parties, and is now in the Posession of the said John Hendricks and of Joshua Minshall, who holds in right of the said James Hendricks; and it appearing to me that the said John Hendricks & Joshua Minshall are settled upon the said Land by regular Surveys ordered to be made in the Year 1728 of which I approve and will order a Patent or Patents to be drawn for that Share of the Land laid out to the said James Hendricks to John Hendricks & Joshua Minshall as soon as the Indian Claim thereon shall be satisfied on the same Terms other Lands in the County of Lancaster shall be granted.
>
> Philadelphia
> 20th March 1732/3

John and James Hendricks' Warrant to settle on West Side Susquehanna River
Original Loose Survey, D-113-181, Pennsylvania State Archives

Land near Conewago and Codorus creeks was attractive for Marylanders and Pennsylvanians alike. Considered to be one of the most fertile areas in Pennsylvania by the *Soil Survey of York County (USDA 15)*, this Conestoga Valley section is an irregular, undulating swath one to four miles wide extending southwest from Wrightsville on the Susquehanna River through the city of York to Hanover. The soil is underlain with limestone, dolomite,

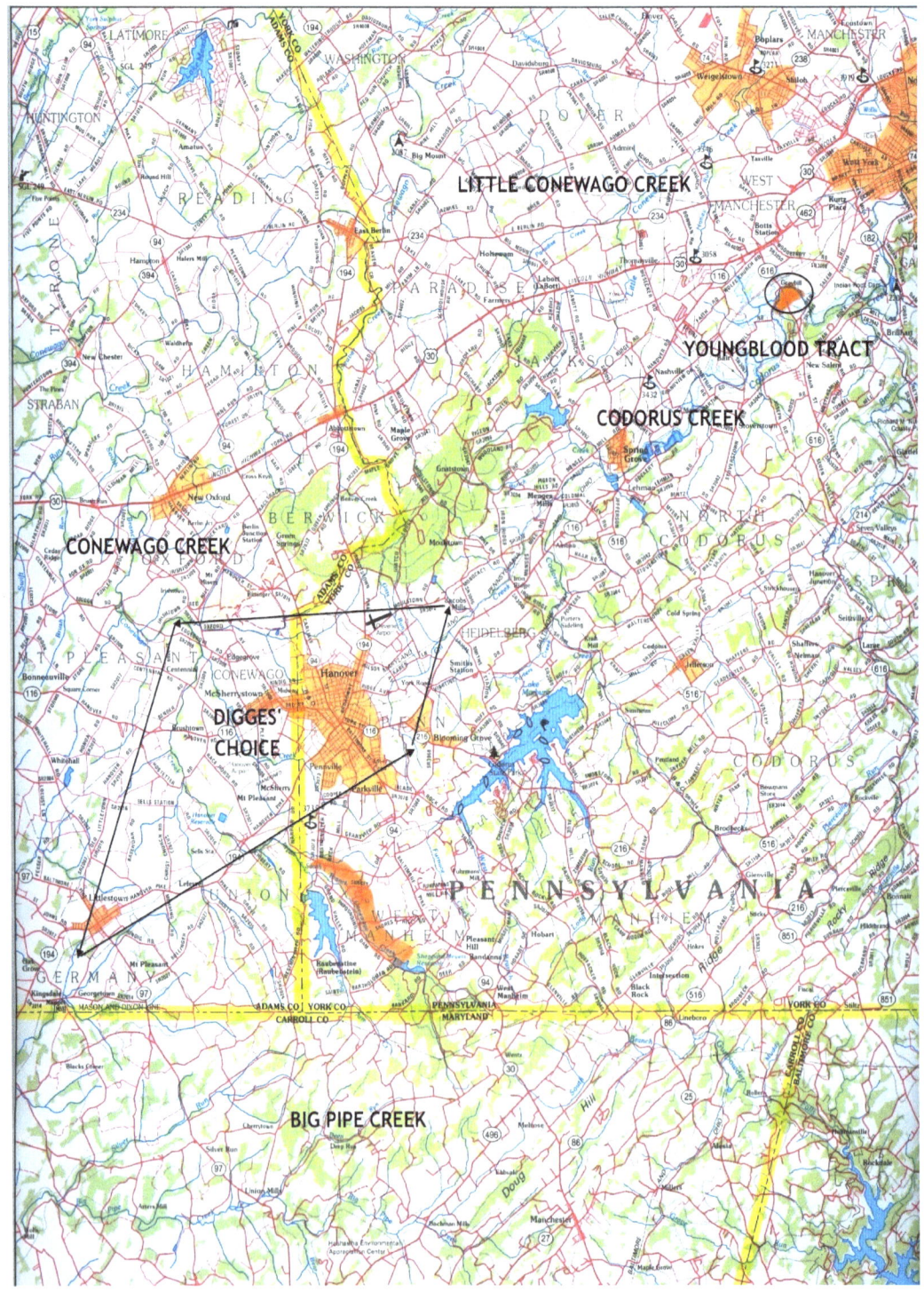

Portions of York, Adams, Carroll counties
Youngblood tract in orange at Graybill,
Digges' Choice and Codorus, Conewago, Little Conewago, and Big Pipe Creeks
Pennsylvania Atlas, DeLorme Mapping

and calcareous schist bedrock and the major streams are Codorus, Kreutz, and Oil Creeks. It is no wonder that Marylanders were as interested as Pennsylvanians in owning land in such a favorable location.

Soon after the 1722 Pennsylvania survey of Springetsbury Manor in this fertile area, Charles Carroll of Maryland, obtained a 1729 Maryland warrant for 10,000 acres lying along Pipe Creek and Conewago and Codorus creeks. While completing the survey in 1732 Carroll and his helper, John Ross, stopped at John Hendricks's home on the Susquehanna. There, a group of Pennsylvanians, some using abusive language, goaded Carroll and Ross to interfere in a Pennsylvania arrest warrant for another Marylander, and expressed resentment of Marylander intrusions above a designated line agreed upon by John, Thomas, and Richard Penn and Lord Baltimore in 1732. *(PA (1): 1: 333-336; Cope 432-441)*

Peter Youngblood's tract lay about 15 miles further west than the Hendricks's home, but on the same Indian trail. Youngblood, himself, may be the Peter Jungbluth who arrived from southwest Germany in 1732. *(Hacker 207)* Peter Youngblood may also have been related to Derrick and Jacob Youngblood, "Dutchmen" who each had tracts at Conewago later on. *(PA (1): 1: 706; Jacob Youngblood, Lancaster County Warrant Register Y 24, 25 Sept 1738)* It is almost certain that this Peter Youngblood is the Peter Youngblood who was naturalized in Maryland March 6, 1739, along with children William, Peter, Sarah, and Mary. Peter Youngblood, a native of Germany, was then a resident of Prince Georges County, Maryland whose jurisdiction extended from the Baltimore County line west. *(Filby from Commission Book 82, Folio 79 Hall of Records, Baltimore, Maryland, in Maryland Historical Magazine. Vol. 26:2 (1931): 155)* Two years later, on March 13, 1741, Peter Youngblood of Prince Georges County, Maryland bought 200 acres on a branch of Great Pipe Creek called "Cattail Marsh" from Michael Resener. Eight years later, Youngblood had the tract resurveyed. *(Jourdan; "Peter Youngblood of Pennsylvania/Maryland.")* Great or Big Pipe Creek is due south of present day Littlestown, Adams County, Pennsylvania.

Land Ownership Troubles

Michael Springle's Blunston/Youngblood tract lay more than 20 miles north of the yet to be surveyed Maryland-Pennsylvania border and outside of Springetsbury Manor, nevertheless he was involved, if only in a minor way, in the developing border dispute. Festering for years, since the beginning of settlement, the border issue had been working its way slowly to a head. Major disagreement existed over certain geographic points and the boundary between the colonies had been surveyed west only to Octorora Creek, the dividing line between Chester and Lancaster counties, not to the Susquehanna River, and definitely not on the west side. *(for a brief yet thorough account see Tittmann)*

Pennsylvania's policy was to prohibit applications for warrants to survey until the proprietors had purchased a given region from the resident Indian landholders. Maryland had no such scruples and was willing to sell land wherever government leaders thought they could secure a toehold. By 1733, a tax collector for Lancaster County reported that there were about 400 tax paying people living in the contested area west of the Susquehanna. *(PA (CR): 3: 477)*

Michael and Anna Margaret were probably already living on their Youngblood tract when skirmishes between settlers from both colonies turned serious the night of January 29, 1733-34 and Knowles Daunt was mortally wounded. Daunt, a Pennsylvanian, was part of a Lancaster County sheriff's posse sent to thwart a group of Marylanders from building a cabin on John Hendricks's land. The Marylanders gathered at Hendricks's clearing early in the day thinking that the land belonged to their friend, William Glasspil. Glasspil, an unsuspecting Marylander, had bought the tract from Thomas Cressap who had an earned reputation as a quarrelsome, Maryland troublemaker. Informed about the intrusion, a Lancaster County sheriff's posse forded the river later in the day, seized and arrested eight Marylanders, and escorted them to jail on the east side of the river. That night, Daunt and his fellow deputies rode after Cressap and found him with several of his men, locked in his own cabin, further south on the Susquehanna near Cabin Creek. Daunt "rudely" approached the cabin and was shot in the leg through a crack in the door. He lay bleeding until morning before rescue. Cressap escaped. Pennsylvania issued a blanket warrant for his arrest. Daunt died in a few days. With his death, the boundary dispute entered a volatile stage. *(Thomas Cressap's surname in his birth country, England, was spelled Crissop. Early Maryland records used Crissop. Pennsylvania records usually used Cressap. Later Maryland records used Cressap. Cresap is usually used today, but to be faithful to the original records and the time, I have used Cressap; PA (1): 1: 410-11; PA (1): I: 412; PA (1): I: 413-14; PA (1): I: 414-17; PA (1): I: 417-23; PA (1): 1: 489)*

Thomas Cressap had lived on 150 acres about midway within Springetsbury Manor along the Susqehanna River since 1729 when he was assigned a Maryland warrant written for Stephen Onion. *(see Map of Springetsbury Manor)* Onion had obtained a Maryland warrant for 500 acres located both north and west of the 150 acres transferred to Cressap, but also within the manor. Other Marylanders also lived within the manor. Philip Syng and Thomas Brown held a 1722 warrant for 200 acres they patented in 1732; John Lowe lived on 372 acres he warranted in 1722 and patented in 1735; and Andrew Maggill had 100 acres assigned to him in 1732 on a warrant originally to Richard Geist also in 1732. *(Hively, Springettsbury 200)* In fact, Lt. Governor Ogle of Maryland encouraged efforts to displace Pennsylvania settlers "in the Northemost Reserve on Susquehannah" and even offered to grant land as a "Gratuity for any services, for any number of Acres to any person" as long as the amount of land did not exceed 1000 acres in any one year, and he pledged that Maryland would collect no money until the boundary was settled. *(Archives of Maryland Online (AOMOL): 39: 507)*

In retribution for Cressap's pursuit, Marylander's apprehended John Hendricks and Joshua Minshall and took them to jail in Annapolis for detention. The men were to be tried by the Maryland Provincial Court on charges of settling and improving land without Maryland approval. *(PA (CR): 3: 542)* While in Annapolis, Hendricks may have decided to support the Marylanders in return for his release. At any rate, Hendricks was released and returned to Pennsylvania to engage in some of the Marylander aggressions. Lancaster County then apprehended and fined him. Utterly unable to pay, he was jailed, but set free in January 1736-7 after posting his future good behavior as security. *(PA (CR): 4: 150)* Deciding that the Cressap situation had gone far enough, Thomas Penn, then Proprietor, sent two emissaries to confer with Deputy Governor Ogle of Maryland. Despite his words to the contrary, Ogle's actions toward the mission showed that he intended to continue to work for Maryland expansion into the area west of the Susquehanna. The emissaries returned to Pennsylvania totally dejected. *(PA (1): 1: 429-33; PA (CR): 3: 547-54)*

Maryland aggressions continued during 1735, but began to come to a head in July 1736 when about "Twenty Men armed with Muskets, Pistols, Blunderbusses & Cutlasses" arrived near the house of John Wright Junior on the Susquehanna to survey land that "long before that time" had been surveyed and settled by Pennsylvanians. The "Captain" of this little venture was none other than Thomas Cressap who, upon questioning, declared that he had orders from Governor Ogle to guard the surveyor as he surveyed all the land between the Susquehanna River and Codorus Creek. During the next four months several Blunston License holders saw portions of their land resurveyed and transferred to Marylanders. Among those affected were some of Michael Springle's neighbors on Codorus Creek such as Frederick Ebert who had settled on the west side of the creek opposite the forks on a November 27, 1734 license granted to Hans Michael Ebert, and Baltzer Spangler whose tract was within Springetsburg Manor in 1736 and who had been there since 1733. *(PA (1): 1: 464-5; PA (1): 1: 519-25; Hively, Springetsbury Map)*

Utterly fed up with "The Oppression & ill Usage" from Maryland, most of the German settlers living on the west side of the Susquehanna River, opposite Hempfield resolved to return their loyalties to Pennsylvania jurisdiction. Proclaiming their original innocence over the location of the boundary between the colonies, but finally realizing that the boundary would be an East-West line, not the North-South Susquehanna River as Marylanders had persuaded them, signed a resolution to live under the laws of Pennsylvania. One copy dated 11 August 1736 went to Maryland's Governor Ogle and one copy dated 13 August 1736 went to Pennsylvania's James Logan and the Council of the Province of Pennsylvania. The petition sent to Maryland claimed forty-eight names; a clerk copied twenty-two names into the record before appending an & al. *(AOMOL: 28: 100-1; PA (CR): 4: 61-2, 64-5)* Michael Springle's name was not one of the twenty-two, but it is probable that it was among the twenty-six left out but under the spelling Michael Arringall. How his name happened to be written "Arringall" or "Aringal" is anyone's guess. The handwritten copy of the Archives of Maryland spells the name with both one and two rs. The printed copy does likewise. Since no census database produces the name Aringall with either one or two rs, we should consider it badly interpreted handwriting, or perhaps entered by someone else who knew of him, only. Later Springle signatures could be misinterpreted, also. Unfortunately, Frederick A. Virkus, editor of *Immigrants to America before 1750*, does include the name Michael

Map showing the area disputed between Maryland and Pennsylvania
Courtesy Cresap's War, Wikipedia, the free encyclopedia

Aringall in his book and assigns the 1736 proclamation date. Since Ancestry.com includes Virkus in its database of Passenger and Immigration Lists Index, 1500s-1900s an unsuspecting researcher could be given a merry chase. However, most Sprinkle/Sprenkle researchers seem to accept that Arringall was poor handwriting for Springle. *(Wentz 203-4)*; Others reported that between fifty and sixty settlers had signed. The petition to Logan claimed forty-eight names. *(PA (CR): 4: 61-2; PA (CR): 4: 56-8; PA (CR): 4: 63-4.)*

No sooner had the German settlers returned their allegiance to Pennsylvania, than the Marylander's mounted an "attack" to avenge the change. Sending two to three hundred well armed men north the first week in September, their goal was to forcibly remove the Pennsylvanians and specifically to take over John Wright Jr.'s settlement. After marching about between John Hendricks and Thomas Cressap's on Sunday the 5th [Julian], blowing trumpets and beating drums, and firing one Blunderbuss toward Pennsylvania reinforcements crossing the Susquehanna, the Maryland force settled in at Cressap's for the night.

Refusing to meet the next day with the sheriff of Lancaster County as planned, the Marylanders took a token prisoner, John Wilkins. Then splitting into two groups, one headed back towards Maryland, the other stopped to plunder, taking cloth from house windows, linens, and pewter as a warning of what would happen if the Germans failed to return to Maryland jurisdiction. *(PA: (1): I: 526-8)* If the Germans would return, the group told Michael Tanner, Maryland would remit their taxes until they were better able to pay and would treat them better in the future. They gave Tanner two weeks to reply. *(PA (CR): 4: 69)*

Marylanders' intrusions drove the Pennsylvania Provincial Council to action. Council members finally realized that controlling the frontier by simply granting warrants to settle was no longer sufficient. Time had come when settler protection was necessary. After the usual political posturing, the Council ordered the Justices and High Sheriffs of Lancaster and Chester counties to be ready with their posses to protect and defend, and to obtain the names of the persons most active in promoting the disturbances. Benjamin Franklin's *Pennsylvania Gazette* published the Proclamation on September 30, 1736. *(PA (CR): 4: 65, 71, 74, 75-79; PA (4): I: 568-69; AOMOL, 28: 99-100; "By the Honorable The...," The Pennsylvania Gazette, September 30, 1736)* Despite a plea from Germans for closer protection than offered, the Council countered by reminding everyone that the Susquehanna River was a great barrier which made a standing militia on the west side impractical. *(PA (CR): 4: 70)* Nevertheless, by the end of September, Pennsylvania had a warrant out for the arrest of Thomas Cressap. *(September 26; PA (1): I: 489)*

Maryland immediately reacted by issuing a proclamation, 21 October 1736 to be exact, for apprehending "all who have acted countenanced or abbetted the Actors in any of the Matters...." Apparently using the names on the resolution they had received from the Germans and adding several more, Maryland came up with a list of sixty to be arrested. This time Michael Springle's name was included, but under the spelling Michael "Aringall." He and fifty others were worth £10 each upon arrest. Michael Tanner, Christian Crowle, and Charles Jones, from the resolution, and Mark Evans and Joshua Minshall, not on the resolution, were worth £20 each. To those, the proclamation added sheriff Samuel Smith, Justice of the Peace Edward Smoutes, Samuel Blunston, and John Wright at a reward of £100 each. Thus, the German signers of the Pennsylvania resolution may have numbered 54 whereas the Maryland Proclamation listed 60. *(Wentz 203-4; AOMOL 28: 100-07)*

While the border dispute between Maryland and Pennsylvania was ongoing, Pennsylvania was also busily involved in negotiations with the Indians of the Five Nations (Onondaga, Seneca, Cayuga, Oneida, Tuscarora) for purchasing the lands lying on both sides of the Susquehanna River. *(The final deed included the Mohawk, thus The Six Nations. PA (1): I: 494-500)* Finalized just ten days before Maryland's arrest proclamation, the 11 October 1736 deed gave

John, Thomas, and Richard Penn, proprietors of Pennsylvania, all the islands lying on the west side of the Susquehanna River to the setting of the sun. Interpreted to be the crest of the Kittatinny Mountains to the west, this deed included land far beyond the German settlers. It also meant that the Pennsylvania land office could begin to accept applications for warrants to survey land on the west side of the Susquehanna River including surveys on Blunston Licenses and on licenses Thomas Penn had signed for land within Springetsbury Manor. Lancaster County warrant registers show that warrants were indeed written, but Michael Springle did not immediately apply for a warrant to have his Youngblood/Blunston tract surveyed.

Returning to the border dispute, Marylanders, including Governor Ogle, had concocted yet another plot to oust the German families from the west side of the Susquehanna River. This plot differed slightly in that Pennsylvanians were the active perpetrators. Henry Munday, Edward Leets, and Charles Higgenbotham of Chester County, acting as agents for Governor Ogle of Maryland and with the full support of Thomas Cressap drummed up a plan to resurvey the tracts originally granted to "Dutch Families" under Maryland warrants and resell them in 200 acre parcels to themselves and forty-nine others. The argument they used was that by returning to Pennsylvania jurisdiction the Germans had disclaimed their right under Lord Baltimore. Learning that Ogle was prepared to send another armed force to protect the surveyors, the Pennsylvania Provincial Council issued warrants for the arrest of Munday, Leets, and Higgenbotham on November 23, 1736. Munday was taken into custody the same day and Leets was also apprehended, but Higgenbotham escaped. He then became the driving force behind even more ruthless tactics against the Germans. *(PA (CR): 4: 100-103)*

A 1736 Chester County court document indicting Henry Munday listed the names of forty-nine early German settlers on the west side of the Susquehanna. These were men who, the list claimed, had been victims of Munday in one way or another. Several of the men's names appeared both on the resolution sent to Maryland announcing their return to Pennsylvania jurisdiction and the petition sent to Pennsylvania asking that they be accepted back. Several, but not all the names also appeared on Maryland's proclamation for apprehension and reward. Other's on the list had given depositions about their plight. Transcription of the names on the Pennsylvania list varies by researcher. Thirty-one had received licenses signed by Thomas Penn in September or October 1736 to settle within Springetsbury Manor. Seventeen of the remaining eighteen had received neither licenses to settle within the manor, nor Blunston Licenses. The one remaining name may have been the only Blunston License holder on the list: Michael Springle. Depending upon researcher, the name was transcribed as Michael Springle, Michael Stringle, Michael Springler, and Michael Spangler, but not Aringall. (*Gibson 602, used both the spelling Springle and Stringle; Bair 178-79 used the spelling Springler; Hively 27 used Spangler on the Pennsylvania List, The Manor of Springetsbury.*)

The day after Munday was captured, Cressap was arrested. Considering that the warrant for Cressap's arrest had been written on September 25 and not acted on until November 24, it can be no coincidence that Cressap was arrested the day after Munday. In the process of taking Cressap, his house was set afire, one of his defenders was killed, and "one gott out at the chimney." Three were sent to the jail in Philadelphia along with Cressap, who was considered to be too dangerous to remain in Lancaster. A sixth, accused of rape in Lancaster County, remained there in jail. Cressap languished in the Philadelphia jail for several months awaiting his release by royal order, a condition that he demanded. *(PA (CR): 4: 109-12; for the Maryland view on Cressap see Wroth)*

While Cressap was in jail, Governor Ogle of Maryland relied on the escaped Charles Higgenbotham for action against the Germans. He appointed Higgenbotham Justice of the Peace and Captain of Militia. Higgenbotham gathered forces and went about threatening, frightening, and destroying German properties. His men took horses and would let no one, not even young boys, plow the fields for spring planting. Then, on December 29, 1736, coming upon six men digging a grave for a child, Higgenbotham and crew seized the men, one was Michael Tanner, and carried them post haste to Annapolis. In his report on the problem and request for aid, Samuel Blunston claimed that many of the German men had fled to the east side of the river leaving only women and children on the west side. *(PA (CR): 4: 147-50, 189; PA (1): 1: 316-20 dated and placed incorrectly as 1732)*

Meanwhile, through letters and depositions, the Pennsylvania Council had learned of Governor Ogle's offer to reward anyone apprehending those listed on his proclamation of 21 October 1736. In Blunston's letter to the Pennsylvania Council, read March 1, 1736-7, he again reminded them "That the large Rewards offered by the Governor of Maryland for apprehending divers of the Magistrates of Lancaster County, as well as others of the Inhabitants living on the east side of the River, have induced several Rogues to come into those parts to attempt something of the kind...." *(PA (CR): 4: 155)* Then, on April 8, the Council learned that the Marylanders intended "in a few days to dispossess" and take over some of the best Pennsylvanian plantations. *(PA (CR): 4: 190)*

Despite the impending threat, the Pennsylvania Council encouraged the Germans to maintain possession of their homes and plantations, suggested lodging a large number of people in John Hendricks' vacant house to defend it vigorously, and recommended asking the sheriff to provide all assistance possible. However, the Council also placed some of the blame on the Germans for their earlier submission to Maryland jurisdiction and for not defending themselves from Maryland aggressions. They pointed out, again, how difficult and expensive it was to defend settlers on the west side of the Susquehanna. Essentially, the Council told the Germans to protect themselves as well as they could until the border issue was settled. *(PA (CR): 4: 194)*

True to its word, Maryland, using Higgenbotham and his followers, carried through on their threat to dispossess some of the Pennsylvanians. On May 18, 1737, Higgenbotham and his friend, Perry, petitioned Governor Ogle for their reward in apprehending twenty-two men named on Ogle's Proclamation. Those arrested had been jailed in Annapolis. Michael Springle's name was not among the twenty-two. Nevertheless, some researchers claim that Michael Springle under the spelling Arringall was one of those apprehended as a result of the Proclamation. For that claim, I have found no proof. *(AOMOL 28: 121-22)*

At the end of May, they were home by June 3, Pennsylvania sent two "Gentlemen" to Annapolis to "press Governor Ogle" on issues for completing a treaty that would stop the disorders on the west side of the Susquehanna. This treaty never happened, but, while in Annapolis, the Gentlemen, Samuel Preston and John Kinsey, had the opportunity for "divers Conferences as well with the Prisoners" and their Counsel about what defense might be necessary against their charges. *(PA (CR): 4: 211)* No further comments about this issue appear in the published Pennsylvania Archives or the Archives of Maryland Online. Presumably the men were released on their own recognizance and the case never went to court.

Perceiving no local resolution to the border issue both Pennsylvania and Maryland, independently, resorted to the King in Council. Each colonial government submitted petitions and depositions to King George II and his Privy Council. Pennsylvania's was composed and sent in December, 1736, after Cressap was jailed, but before Higgenbotham began his attacks. *(PA (CR): 4: 124-29)* Maryland sent her petition in February 1736-7. *(AOMOL 28: 110-18)*

Almost a year went by before the colonies received their responses. Arriving in the form of a preliminary order only, dated August 18, 1737, Maryland received her copy first in November 1737. *(AOMOL 28: 130; 40: 585-86)* Pennsylvania received her copy at the beginning of January 1737-8 and immediately ordered it published as a Proclamation which the Pennsylvania Gazette did on January 17. *(PA (CR): 4: 262)* Final Orders in Council arrived respectively in May and August 1738. *(PA (CR): 4: 297; AOMOL, 28: 145-48)* An important condition for the settlers was that warrants to survey dated before the date of the preliminary order were deemed legal regardless of location. As far as the border was concerned, the two colonies working together were to run a temporary line on the west side of the Susquehanna fourteen and three-quarters miles south of the latitude of the most southern part of the city of Philadelphia. *(PA (CR): 4: 300)* In May, 1739 surveyors completed the temporary line between the two colonies. That line approximated the final surveying of the line which occurred a generation later between 1763 and 1767. Following the preliminary order in 1737 many Germans applied for warrants to survey the tracts they were on, or for new warrants for vacant land. Still others became involved in legal battles over the determination of warrant priority. Michael Springle, however, had no more involvement in the border affair.

Transportation, Taxes, and Another Tract

Michael and Anna Margaret and the other German families living on the west side of the Susquehanna River could now concentrate on developing their farms and their home life. When he bought the Youngblood property, Michael knew exactly what he was looking for. Not only did he want more acreage than his Conestoga tract, he wanted a tract heavily timbered with hardwoods, with banked meadows, and a rich, light soil, free from ponds and stagnated water, along a stream and an old Indian trail. Germans usually looked for soil that produced hardwoods knowing that it was more fertile and would produce larger crops. *(Long 2)* Michael intended to raise flax and hemp, two of the most useful plants in colonial Pennsylvania.

Hemp was particularly needed in the ship building industry for making strong, durable cordage and cables and England provided a ready market. Beginning in 1722 and continued in 1725, Pennsylvania subsidized hemp growing by offering one penny per pound on "good, sound, well-dressed, merchantable hemp, suitable and fit for export." *(PSL 3 St.L. 314, Ch. 257; 4 St.L. 30, Ch. 286)* Within a few years, the subsidy generated a serious problem in the quality of hemp being brought to market in Philadelphia, so in 1727 the Assembly raised the subsidy to "one penny half penny for every pound" and added an additional clause requiring subsidized hemp to be "water-rotted and dried, without the help of fire." *(PSL 4 St.L. 68, Ch. 294)* The increased allowance "much encouraged many people within this province to apply themselves to the raising of good hemp and carefully to water-rot the same," but, apparently, inspection was lacking. Thus, in February 1729-30, the Assembly passed yet another hemp act. This law extended the subsidy, or bounty, of one penny half penny per pound for water-rotted hemp fit for exportation and delivered to the "public beam at the workhouse in Philadelphia," but required that it undergo inspection and the seller take an oath or affirmation that the hemp was grown in Pennsylvania before it could be sold. Hemp that did not pass inspection was forfeited, paid for at value, and delivered to the workhouse for their use. *(PSL 4 St.L. 184, Ch. 316)*

Michael would have been aware of this most favorable treatment for hemp. Perhaps he had been growing hemp in Conestoga Township. As late as 1747, Benjamin Franklin had written the Reverend Jared Elliot in Connecticut that the greater part of Pennsylvania hemp was brought from Conestoga in wagons to Philadelphia. *(Stark10)* Michael would also have known that by 1731 the demand for water-rotted hemp had risen to the point where the subsidy was not necessary and the Pennsylvania Assembly had repealed the premium effective July 1, 1732. *(PSL 4 St.L. 231, Ch. 328)* Nevertheless, Michael may have thought that the price of hemp was high enough to bring him a good profit wherever he sold.

Ferry Scene on the Susquehanna at Wright's Ferry
Painting by Pavel Petrovich Svinin, 1811 - 1813
© Metropolitan Museum of Art
Courtesy scholarsresource.com

Transportation costs, of course, would diminish the profit. From Conestoga to Philadelphia was a distance of about 80 miles. Michael now lived another 25 miles west, making his trip to Philadelphia about 100 miles. With a river to cross, travel expenses were even greater. Wright's Ferry was the only commercial way to cross the wide, shallow Susquehanna River. Opened in 1730, the ferry first amounted to two dugout canoes fastened together with carriage and wagon wheels. People and goods rode onboard, but the river was shallow enough during certain times of the year for large farm wagons to ford and certain livestock to walk, provided they were guided. Fare prices from the 1730s and 1740s are not known. The fee structure quoted online dates from a later era when coaches and Conestoga wagons could fit on a larger ferry.

It is no wonder that one of the first concerns of settlers on the west side of the Susquehanna was improved transportation. Most Blunston License holders held tracts on one side or the other of the old Indian trail to the Monocacy River. *(Hively, Springetsbury Map)* In 1739, several families living along the trail on the west side of the Susquehanna in newly formed Hellam Township petitioned the Lancaster County Court of Quarter Sessions to view and lay out a road from Wright's Ferry on the Susquehanna to the Potomac River. These settlers envisioned improving the old Indian trail that ran by their tracts as far as the Monocacy

Road from Susquehanna to Monocacy
Lancaster County Court Docket 1, 1729-1742, LancasterHistory.org

and on to the Potomac. Court appointed surveyors from the township reported in February 1740, not surprisingly, in favor of the route. They suggested that the road begin at the Susquehanna between the lands of John Wright, Jr. and Samuel Taylor, run south and west to Big Codorus Creek, to "Springlers field," continue south, west, and southwest to the West Branch of Codorus Creek and so on. *(Court Docket No. 1, 1729 - 1742. LancasterHistory.org; Nead 47)* This route became the Monocacy Road. Much later the Monocacy Road became the Lincoln Highway, and still later US Highway 30. Hively's map leaves no doubt, "Springler's field" belonged to Michael Springle.

For a few years, 1739 to 1742, Hellam Township, or Hallam as later spelled, was the only township on the west side of the Susquehanna and covered much of the area that later became York County. Before 1739 Hempfield Township opposite on the east side of the Susquehanna had jurisdiction. The Pennsylvania Provincial Assembly had not given Lancaster County authority to form townships west of the Susquehanna until the Indian purchase treaty was approved and border problems with Maryland had been settled. By 1739 residents were eager for local government and the population was large enough to support it. Even the constable for Hempfield Township, Charles Jones, lived on the west side of the Susquehanna. Since it was his lawful duty to enumerate all residents annually for tax assessment, we know that the west side residents were all assessed even though "the levying of them" was "deferred till the Limits were adjusted." (PA (CR): 4: 200)

Lancaster County first assessed taxes for Hellam Township in 1741. Even then the residents of Hellam were so poor that the total assessment amounted to only £3.12.8. Only a small portion of Michael's property lay within a bend of Codorus Creek in Hellam Township. Two other townships, Manchester and Pennsboro, both formed from Hellam, were also assessed for the first time in 1741. The much larger portion of Michael's land including the largest fields lay within Manchester Township. *(Hively, Springetsbury Map)* Manchester's assessment totaled £5.13.10 or 1366d, and Pennsboro's was set at £11.15.10. Hellam Township was named after Hallam, the township in England where Samuel Blunston was born. Unfortunately, no list of individual taxpayers survives, but the aggregate tax for each Lancaster County township does survive for the period 1729-30 - 1749. The tax collector's name and pay and accounts associated with tax collecting survive, likewise. *(Lancaster County, Minute Book and Tax Notes 1729 - 1844)*

To place the assessments for the new townships in perspective, in 1742 the valuation rates in Lancaster County were £6 per hundred acres for land from the lower end of the county to Chiquesalunga (now Chiques) Creek just south of Marietta and £4 for land north of Chiquesalunga Creek. The rate schedule did not mention land tax on the west side of the Susquehanna River. Valuation on other property was assessed at 5s per acre for winter grain; £2 per head for horses and mares; £1 per head for cows; £1/8 per head for sheep; £3 each for White servants; £10 each for Negroes. Since the bulk of Michael's land lay in Manchester Township he was assessed there as a resident. Although only the aggregate township tax survives, the assessment rate was the same as in 1726-7. If the valuations were similar, 26 or 27 taxpayers would make up the £5.13.10 aggregate tax for Manchester for 1741-2. Figure it this way: Michael's tax in Conestoga Township 1726-7 = 4s 3d = 51d; total Manchester tax in 1741-2 = £5.13.10 = 1366d. Dividing the total Manchester tax by Michael's tax (1336 ÷ 51= 26.19) equates to 26 or 27 taxpayers. Undoubtedly Manchester had at least or more residents than that. So, although we do not have individual rates, we do know that Michael and his neighbors had greatly reduced their tax liability by moving west. Rates were not increased until 1750 when York County was formed and had 1466 taxable properties. *(Lancaster County, Pennsylvania. Minute Book and Tax Notes 1729 - 1844)*

Residents could appeal their assessment, but appeals were heard on one day, only, at the Court House in Lancaster on the east side of the Susquehanna. To get to the Court House meant traveling to either Anderson's (1742) or Wright's (1730) ferry, perhaps staying in their tavern overnight, paying the ferry fee, then walking or riding on to the town of Lancaster, another 12 miles or so. This might take two days. A third day would be needed for the appeal's hearing and then a minimum of another day or two for the trip home. Under these conditions it would not have been cost effective to appeal.

The formation of Hellam, Manchester, and Pennsboro Townships shows how rapidly the west side was filling up. Before all the good land ended up in private hands, the Penns issued Thomas Cookson, deputy surveyor for Lancaster County, a warrant "to survey and lay off in lots a tract of land on the Codorus where the Monocacy Road crosses the stream" for the new proprietary town of York. Presumably, this location was within the 1722 survey of Springetsbury Manor for it was a new idea of the younger Penn's to create proprietary towns within their manors or in key locations. *(Munger 88)* This first plat of York Town Cookson did in October 1741 with the assistance of Baltzer Spangler and Ulrich Wissler both of whom held licenses for tracts within the manor. Much to the surprise of everyone, George Stevenson's 1754 resurvey showed that the 436.5 acres surveyed for York Town lay about 1.5 miles outside the Manor to the west. Michael's tract lay another four miles west.

Within a month after Cookson's original survey, twenty-three persons had applied for lots in York Town. Two years later, October 1743, York Town had eleven houses and applications for church lots from both the Lutheran and Reformed congregations. Residents had also opened a road to Baltimore, then called Potapsco, only 45 miles away compared to the 90 miles and "ye Ferriage over ye Susquehanna." The prospect of York becoming a county seat pleased many traders and speculators alike. *(Gibson, 514-15)*

Cookson, as deputy surveyor for Lancaster County, was responsible for all the surveys on the west side of the Susquehanna 1741 through 1749. After Samuel Blunston's death in 1745 Cookson inherited his papers including his record book of licenses to settle. Evidence indicates that Cookson surveyed Michael Springle's Blunston/Youngblood tract in April 1746. A resurvey of Michael's tract in 1767 names Cookson as the original surveyor. Neighbor George Myer's Blunston tract was definitely surveyed on April 18, 1746, as also was Myer's neighbor Michael Ebert's. *(Myer, Copied Survey B-12-223; Ebert, Copied Survey B-3-54)* None of these Cookson surveys, York Town, Springle, Myer, nor Ebert, and undoubtedly many others, was recorded in the proprietary land office then located in Philadelphia. *(Min-*

utes of the Provincial Council, November 22, 1738. PA (CR): 4: 313; Hively, Springettsbury 35-8; Gibson 514-16; Munger, 88-9; Copied Survey B-5-19)

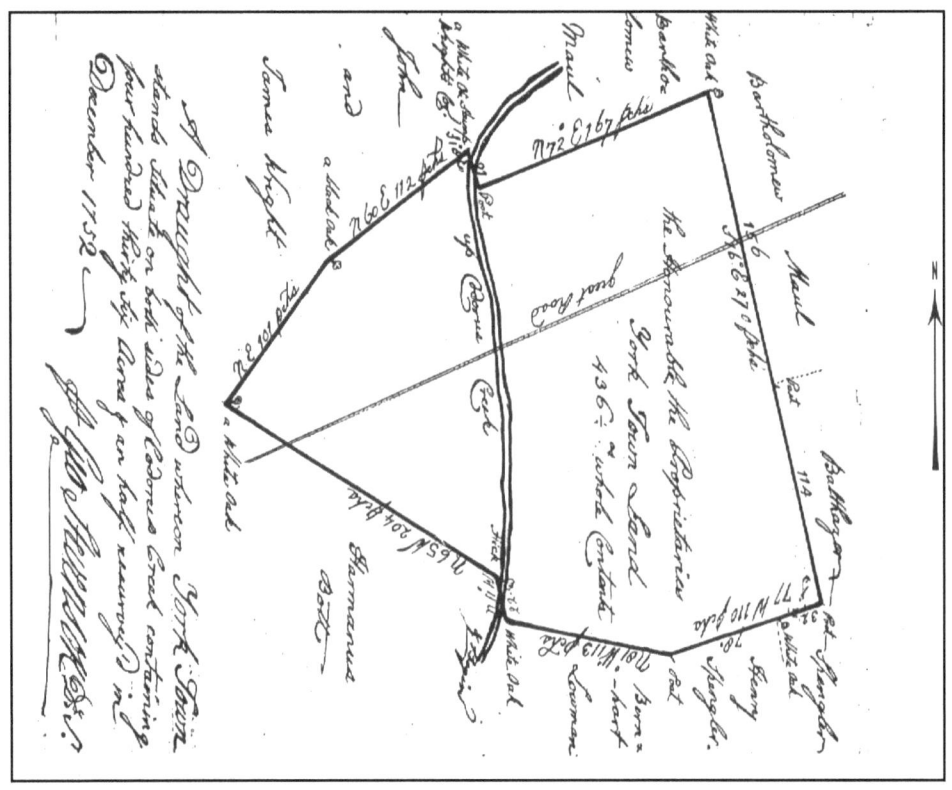

Survey of York Town
Copy of Stevenson's 1752 resurvey using Cookson's metes and bounds.
Diagram on side to show directions: arrow points north
Original and Copied Surveys D-83-16, Pennsylvania State Archives

It is likely that upon finding out that he did not own as much land on both sides of Codorus Creek as he wanted, Michael Springle applied in October 1746 for an additional 200 acres adjacent southwest of his original tract. *(Lancaster County Warrant Register S 498 p. 200)* Straddling Codorus Creek, the new tract lay in Hellam Township, but in 1747 fell under the jurisdiction of Codorus Township when Codorus was incorporated from Hellam. Michael did not pursue the patenting process. He should have paid one half of the purchase price of £15.10 per 100 acres, or at least a minimum of £5 per 100, to obtain the warrant to survey. *(Munger 57, 81; Shepherd 34)* The tract would then be his provided he improved and cultivated the land. Although York Deed F-256 gives a date of April 13, 1747 for the survey, York survey 5404 claims that only a rough draught and calculation of 199 acres 34 perches was then done. *(York Survey 5404; Hively, Springetsbury 75)*

Lancaster County Warrant Register, page 200
Pennsylvania State Archives

On the same October day, William Springle also applied for and received a warrant for his own tract of one hundred acres. *(Lancaster County Warrant Register S 507)* This was no coincidence. Applications needed to be presented in writing to the land office in Philadelphia. Either Michael and William traveled to Philadelphia together, or someone like deputy surveyor Cookson submitted the applications for them. As the first step in the patenting process, the land office filed applications separately and many still exist. *(Munger, 106-7)* Probably William had been living on the tract he applied for as a presumptive settler; that would not have been unusual.

Located due south of York Town, William's tract was located similarly to Michael's. His acreage lay on both sides of a bend of the South East Branch of Codorus Creek and on both sides of the Old Trail from York to Baltimore. Michael lived five and one-third miles to the northwest as the crow flies. When first surveyed in 1752, William's tract contained not one hundred acres, but two hundred forty-four acres. William was liable to pay for that amount if he chose to patent the tract, but he did not pursue the patent.

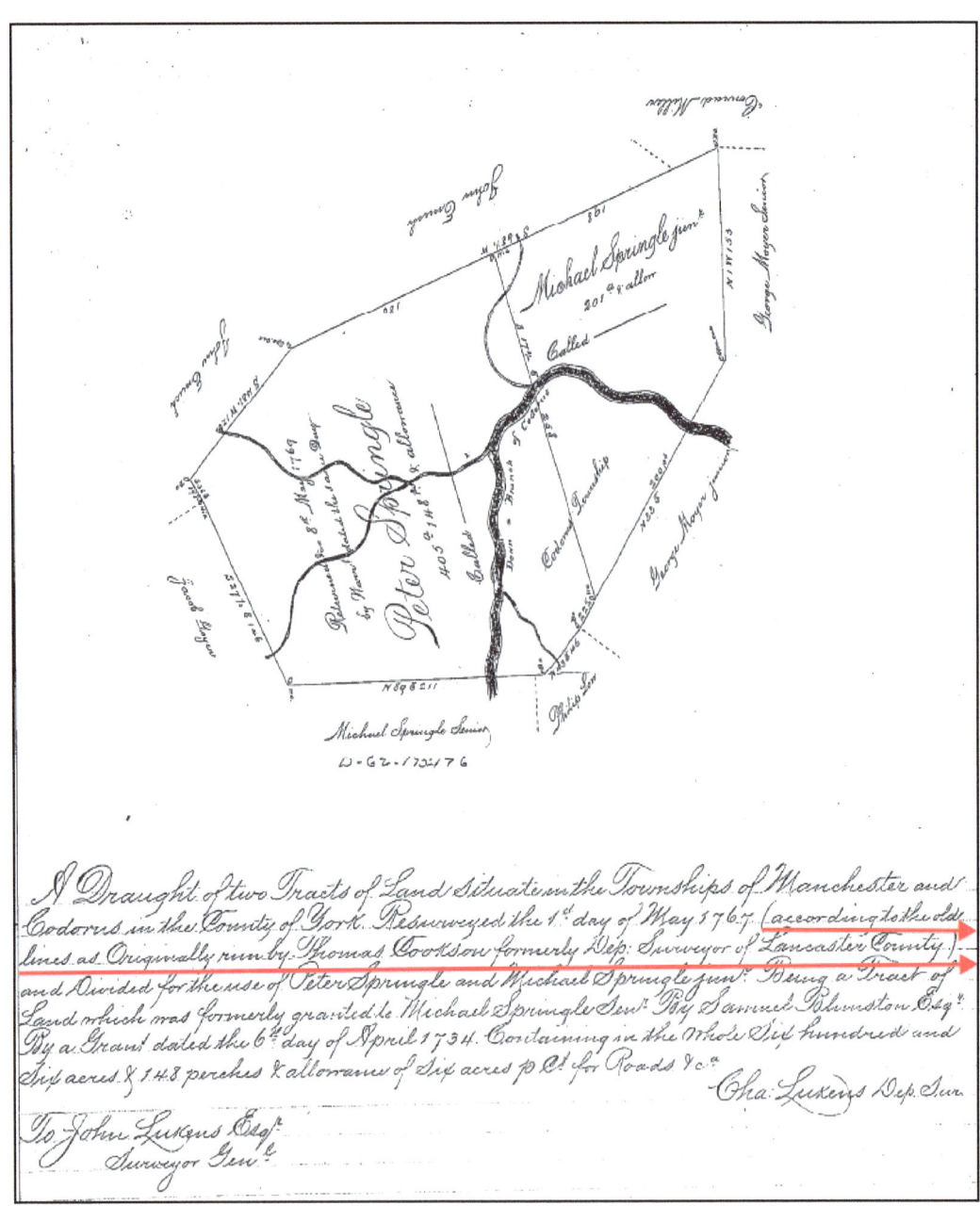

Michael Springle's Blunston Tract
As originally surveyed by Cookson, the tract contained 500 acres,
not the 600 acres recorded in this survey of 1767.
The official division between Peter and Michael junr. dates from 1762.
Copied Survey B-5-19, Pennsylvania State Archives

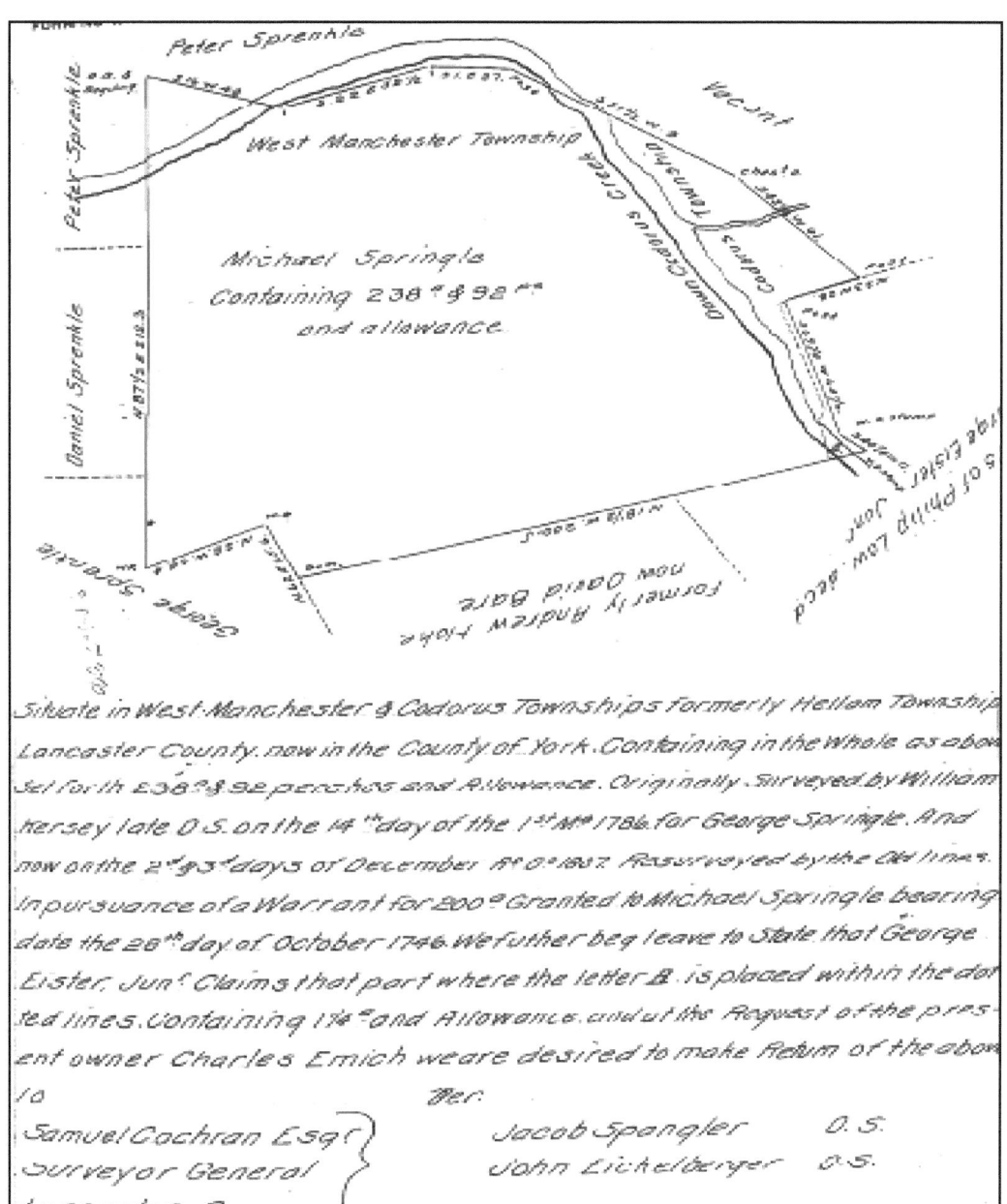

Michael Springle's 1746 Warrant Tract
Left side faces north and adjoins Michael Springle's Blunston Tract
Copied Survey D-62-175, Pennsylvania State Archives

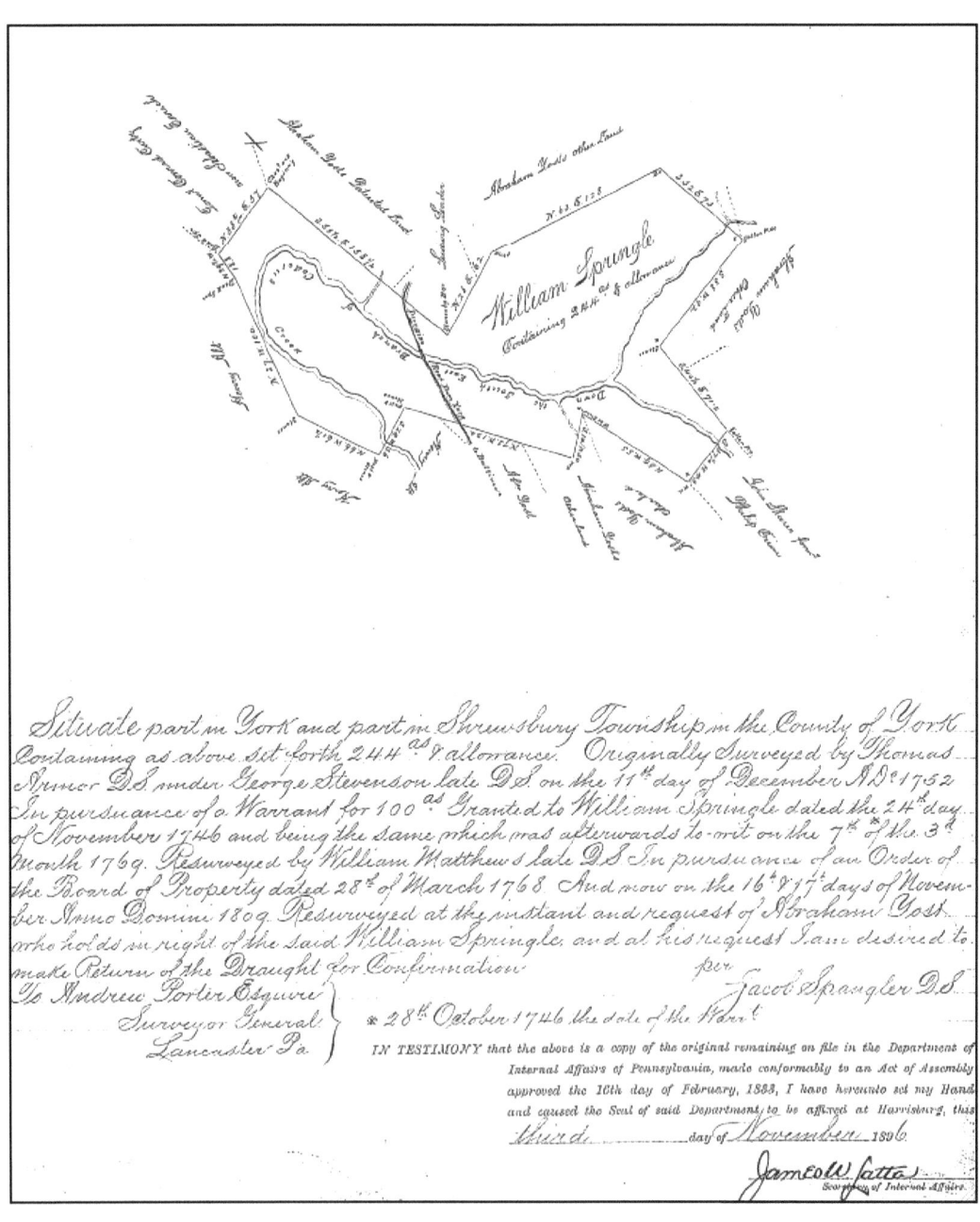

William Springle's 1746 Warrant Tract
Copied Survey B-1-5, Pennsylvania State Archives

William Springle's 1746 Warrant Tract (1168) and his 31 acre West Side Application 4817 Tract (1743) outlined in red on Neal Hively's York Township Warrant Tract map. Green dot dash line marks boundary between York Township and Springetsbury Manor. Match Jacob Fleeger tract on both maps for relative location of Michael Springle and William Springle. Note how each man selected land on both sides of deep bends in creeks.

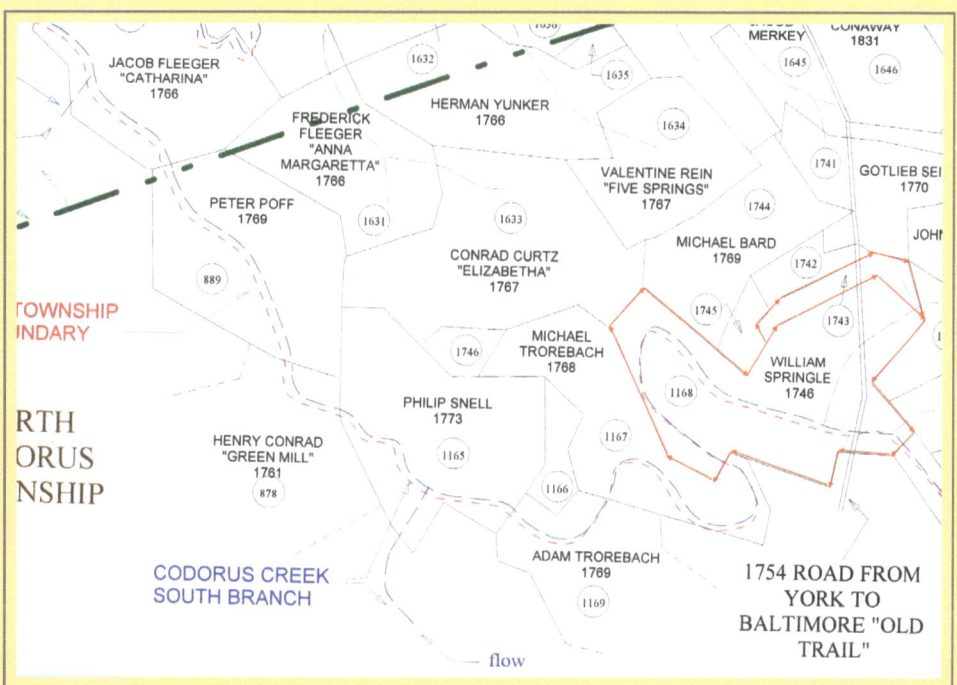

William died in 1772. His Will was dated 16 January and proved 11 April. Wife, Catharine, was living as were his twelve grown children. From William's Inventory taken 4 April, we can tell that he was a retired farmer. For example, he had a side saddle and a man's saddle, but only one colt. His only obvious farm activity was caring for 15 sheep, a horn cattle, and a few small swine. His house and farm Inventory plus notes, bonds, and other debt owed to him totaled £181.8.2. Following the terms of his Will, William's property was sold and his estate was settled 7 June 1774. Catharine received one-third of the estate balance. The remaining two-thirds was "equally divided among" the children "So that no one" of his "children have or receive more than the other according to my Will and Intent."

William Springle/Sprenckel Estate Papers. York County Archives

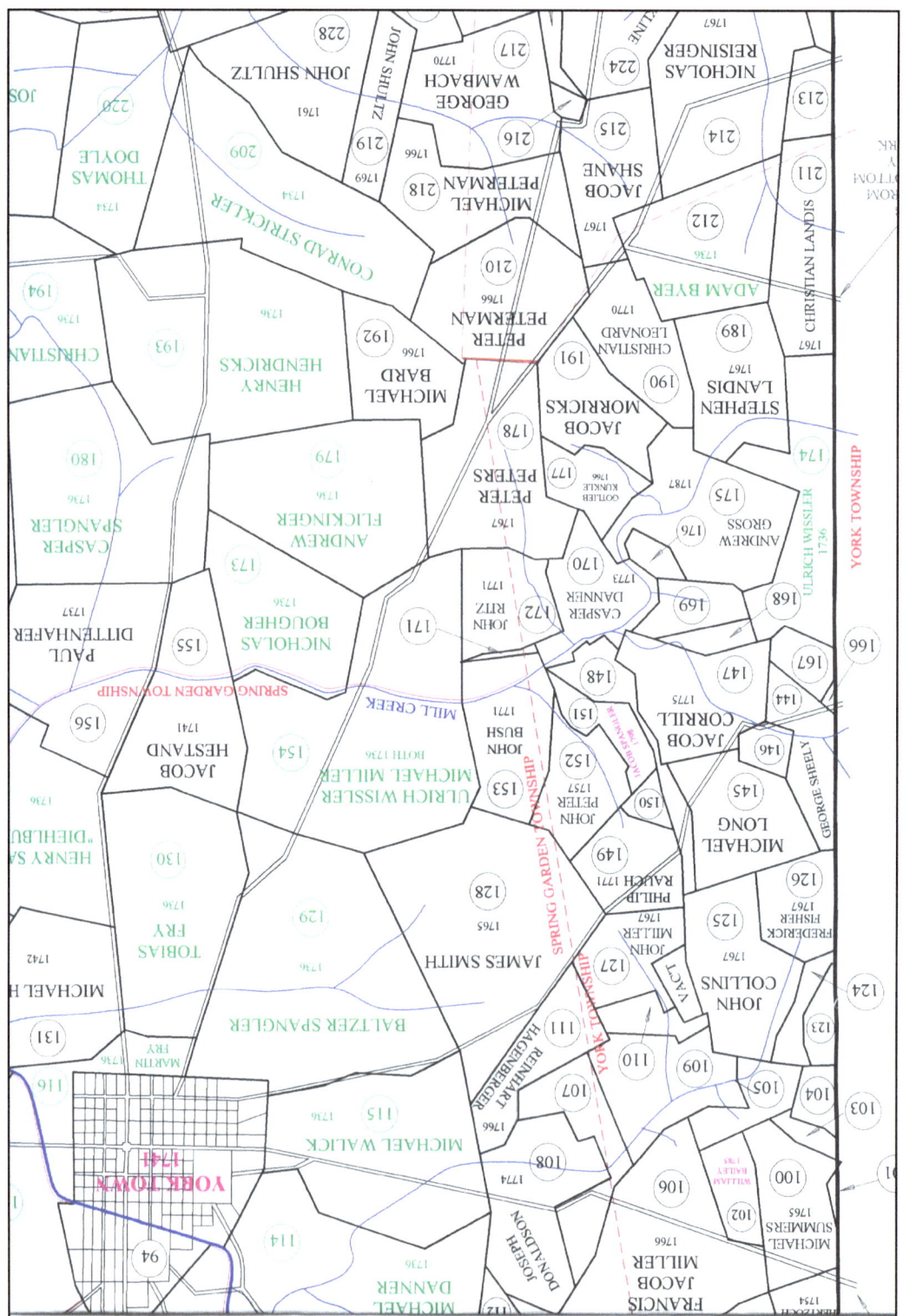

The Manor of Springetsbury
Connected Warrant Tract Map, survey of 1768, east section
This and next section join. Top of pages are east, left sides are north

Michael Springle in Pennsylvania   49

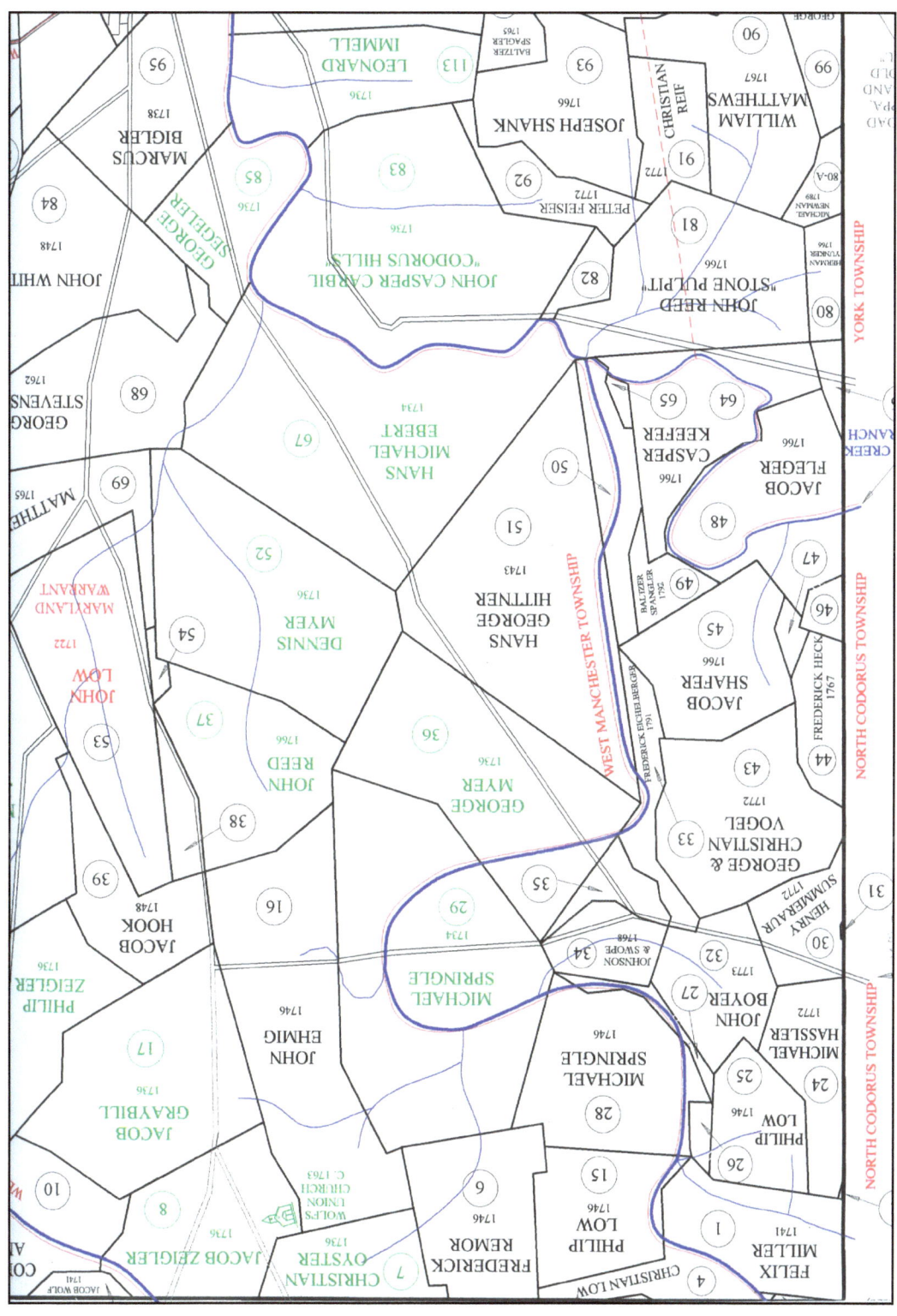

The Manor of Springetsbury
Connected Warrant Tract Map, survey of 1768, west section
Courtesy Neal Otto Hively

Farm, Home, and Family Life

Michael and Anna Margaret spent the rest of the time they had together, in Manchester Township, Lancaster County. No records for Michael will be found in York County, only records for Anna Margaret and their children. As a couple, Michael and Anna Margaret worked diligently to develop their farm while raising a family of fourteen children, twelve of whom lived a full life. The inventory of Michael's estate taken after his death, the administration of his accounts, and a whole host of later family deeds all divulge a great deal about Michael and Anna Margaret's life. Coupled with other documents and sources and compared to other individuals who lived in the area at the same time, quite a complete picture develops.

In the twenty years or so that they lived on the west side of the Susquehanna, Michael and Anna Margaret had amassed a net worth of £716.3.4. Michael had become a wealthy farmer. His holdings were far larger than the average Lancaster County farm of 125 acres. *(Lemon 71-97, Table 27)* Michael had warrant rights to 700 acres: the 500 acre Blunston tract and the 200 acre 1746 tract. The administration of his accounts completed 6 June 1749 showed a gross valuation of £754.4.8 and debts of £38.1.4. His greatest debts were to son for Peter £4.17, neighbor George Myers £4.2.6, fulling mill owner Matthew Atkinson £2.16.8, and John Road for £2.11.2. Of the other 22 people his usual debt was less than one pound.

When Michael died in 1748 he had winter grain in his "upper Improvement" and on "The Big Plantation." This may have been entirely wheat or a combination of wheat, barley, and rye, grains used primarily for family consumption and animal feed. He may also have sold some on the local market. Throughout the early colonial period, wheat and flour were Pennsylvania's main exports. Wheat required little work to sow and Michael owned "two old plows and Harrow" that could have turned the soil, but heavy labor was needed for harvesting because the grain ripened within a very short period. Michael probably produced only what his family and a few helpers could cut, an average of 10 bushels per acre, using the "10 Sickles" inventoried. *(Lemon, 152; Purvis, Colonial America, 77-8)*

Besides winter grain, Michael raised hemp and flax. When he died he had £40 worth of fresh hemp on hand. Bezanson et al. in *Prices in Colonial Pennsylvania 76,* also *Purvis 63* tell us that hemp fluctuated between 3 and 4 pence a pound in 1749. Using the 4 pence quote, Michael's £40 or 9600d worth of hemp meant he had 2400 pounds in stock. His well-drained lowlands, especially in the bend of the Codorus, would have been ideal for growing hemp as hemp likes soil with a high moisture content. Statistics in *Colonial America to 1763 (Purvis, 63)* claim that a farmer could care for 4 acres of hemp and get a yield of

1000 pounds per acre. Lemon's hypothetical production based on his Lancaster County research more conservatively figured a yield of 300 pounds per 2 acres. Using Lemon's estimate, Michael might have had as many as 16 acres in hemp production. *(Lemon, Table 27: 152)* For flax, Lemon showed about the same, but for flaxseed, he figured about 5 bushels per 2 acres. Michael's 10 bushel's of flaxseed were valued at only £1 for all. Each bushel was therefore worth 24 pence or 2 shillings each, or about half of the average price on export from Philadelphia to Ireland in the 1740s. *(Bezanson, 67-8)*

Hemp and flax were labor intensive crops. James Wright of Hempfield Township, Lancaster County explained in an article published in Benjamin Franklin's *Poor Richard's Almanac* in 1765 how farmers grew hemp in Lancaster County. First, the soil needed to be broken in the fall and twice plowed in the spring, the second time just before the seed was sown which needed to be done during the first half of May. A bushel and a peck of good seed planted one acre. After seeding, the field was harrowed smooth. With his "two old plows and Harrow" Michael could have done the planting. Nothing more needed to be done until the crop was ready for pulling, then it was a multistep process similar to preparing flax for spinning. Pulling literally meant pulling the hemp from the ground, roots and all and beating off the soil. Next came retting, or spreading the stalks carefully on the ground for about a week until dry. Dry stalks were bound in sheaves and several sheaves stacked together in tepee form for further drying. When totally dry, the hemp was stacked in a hemp house or in long covered batches outdoors with roots all in one direction until mid November. Then, the hemp was spread in thin, even rows in a closed field, for watering, until about the middle of March when the hemp was ready for breaking, or shaking out. Most Pennsylvania farmers used an inexpensive braking machine that allowed one person to do a rough break on the root end followed by cleaning and finishing on the top part without laying down the bundle so that the hemp came out clean and the silk or harl remained strong. Hemp that went to market was then packed in tight bundles of 100 to 150 pounds each. Hemp for home use might be draped over a skutching board and beaten with a wooden skutching knife to clean it a second time. Scutched hemp might then be taken to a mill for more softening by stamping or rolling to break down the resinous coating and subdivide the fibers. Michael had a "Grain Stone." Perhaps he used that to softened his hemp. The closest hemp mills were on the east side of the Susquehanna, a long and expensive trip. Some authorities suggest that cider mills could soften hemp and crush flaxseed for linseed oil. Wright implies that many farmers did not use hemp mills, but went directly to hackling or combing the fibers through an iron spiked board, called a hatchel. Finally, the hemp was ready for spinning. *(Stark 13-6; Litchfield 51-4)*

Farmers grew, harvested, and prepared flax in almost the same way. Both crops drained the soil of nutrients so some farmers rotated with winter wheat. Perhaps that is why Michael's inventory showed that both the upper Improvements and the Big Plantation contained winter wheat; or perhaps the unplanted Lower Improvement valued at only £5.0.0 was to be planted using some of the flax seed. Three pecks to an acre yielded from six to twelve bushels of seed. With his ten bushels, Michael could have planted thirteen acres, or he could have been planning to take the seed to the mill to be made into linseed oil which could be used for waterproofing fabric, as an emollient, or even as a gentle laxative. *(Keller 266-273)*

For spinning his hemp, flax, and wool from his 25 sheep, Michael owned "a Bik Spinen Wheel" and "4 Spinnen Wheels," enough spinning wheels to keep his four oldest daughters and Anna Margaret busy on long, winter evenings. The four smaller spinning wheels were probably treadle driven, saxony wheels that used a flyer and bobbin to spin flax and hemp thread and wind it onto a bobbin. The long, finished flax fibers were placed on a distaff that was attached to, or stood next to the spinning wheel and secured with a ribbon to hold the fiber in place while spinning. Spinners usually kept their fingers wet while spinning to achieve a smoother, softer yarn and manipulate the ends of the fibers into the twist. After filling several bobbins, the finished thread was wound into a skein on a clock reel or on a "niddy noddy." Skeins could be washed or dyed, then wound into balls for knitting or on to bobbins or shuttles for weaving. Some thread was suitable for making fine linen while other was used for making tough, durable work clothes, grain bags, and the like. *("Colonial American Spinning & Weaving"; PippiKneeSocks)* Michael's "Bik Spinen Wheel" was probably used for wool. It was of older design than the saxony wheel, and was also called a walking wheel because the spinner needed to walk back and forth in front of the wheel while spinning.

Pennsylvania German Seated Spinning Wheel
Pennsylvania German Society Schantz, insert, 26-7

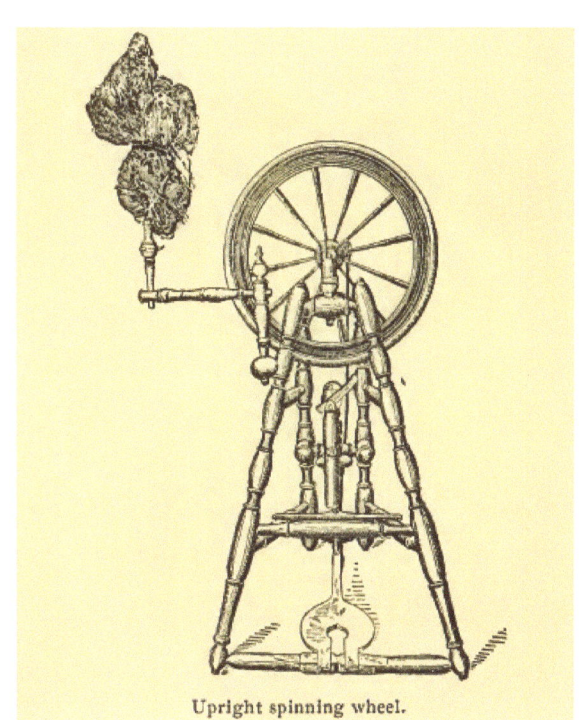

Pennsylvania German Upright Spinning Wheel
Pennsylvania German Society Schantz, insert, 26-7

Michael did not have a loom, so we know that he took some of his hemp and flax thread to a weaver where it was woven into cloth. Other thread he might have sold or traded. After Michael's homespun thread or yarn had been woven, the cloth would go to the fulling mill to be washed, dyed, and spread to shrink and dry. In the process, the loose fibers would become entangled in one another and fill up the spaces between the warp and weft making a much stronger and better appearing fabric. *(For a good, brief explanation of fulling see Glover Fulling Mill. Haddon Heights Historical Society.)* Perhaps Michael used Matthew Atkinsons' fulling mill, hence the £2.16.8 debt. The mill was situated on Conestoga Creek about eight miles upstream from Michael's original tract and very near the old road from Philadelphia to Lancaster. Matthew had inherited the mill from his father, Stephen Atkinson, a clothier, in 1742. (Atkinson, Stephen. Will, Book A1-72. Lancaster County Archives) Michael would have approached the mill from the west taking the Monocacy Road from his plantation to Wright's Ferry on the Susquehanna, then the Conestoga Road through the town of Lancaster to the mill. In today's Lancaster, the Atkinson Fulling Mill would be in the southeast quadrant.

Stephen Atkinson had received a warrant to build his fulling mill and a dam on Conestoga Creek August 27, 1728, agreeing to pay £25 per hundred acres and 1 shilling sterling quitrent annually. Little did he know that his mill would be involved in one of the earliest environmental controversies in Pennsylvania. Surveyed within the month by John Taylor, Atkinson's mill tract lay within a sharp bend of Conestoga Creek and contained 138 acres.

To protect his mill dam, he was allowed seven acres to the east opposite the dam, but environmentalists were active then, as now. Complaints about the dam were soon expressed. In

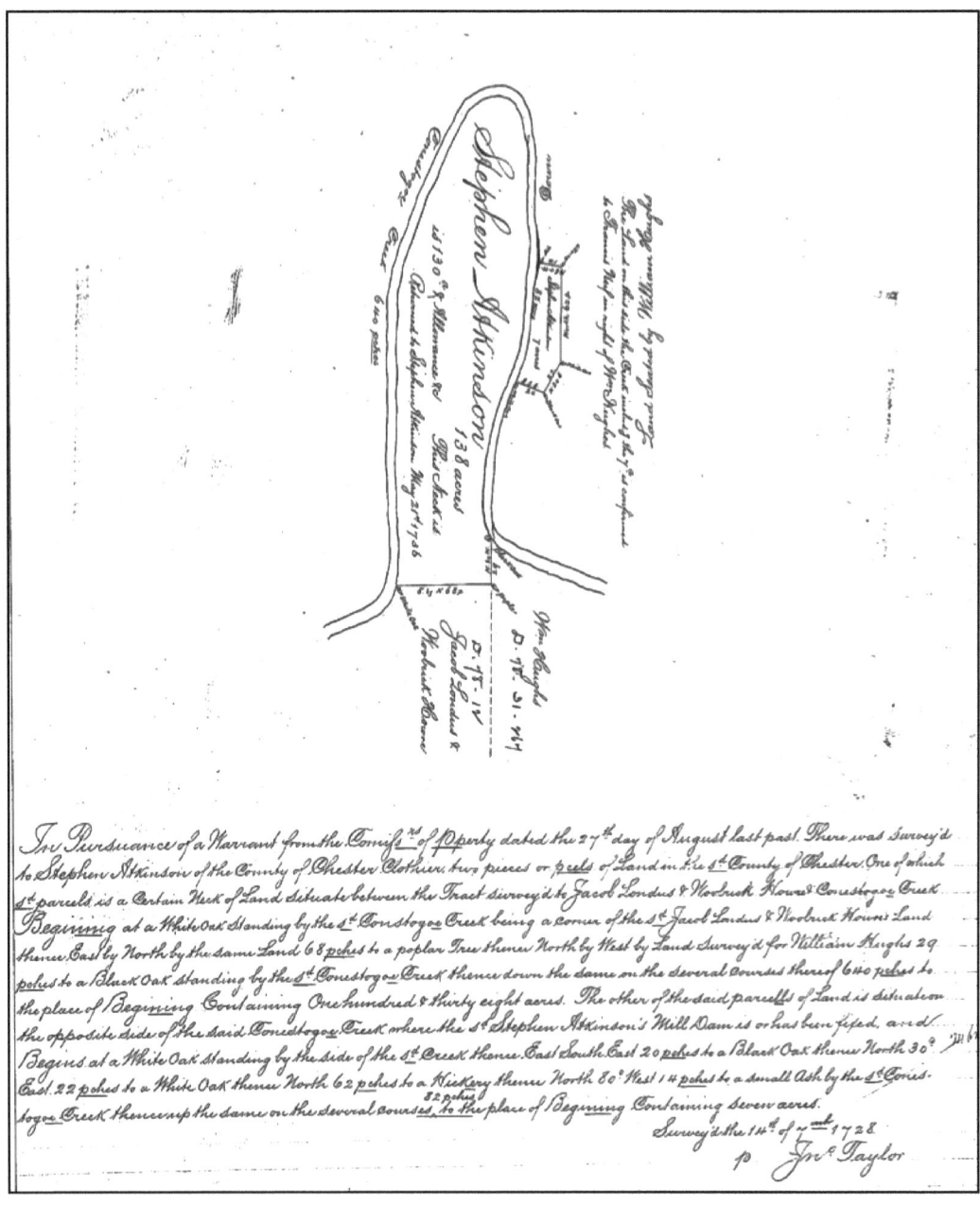

Stephen and Matthew Atkinson's Fulling Mill tract on Conestoga Creek
Copied Survey B-6-5, Pennsylvania State Archives

January 1730-31, several residents brought a petition to the Provincial Assembly alleging that the dam deprived them of "great Quantities of Fish" and prevented them from using the creek for *"transporting their Commodities."* (PA (8): 3: 2048) Atkinson had his chance to defend himself on Monday, August 2, 1731, when he appeared before the House. In humble

Michael Springle's Conestoga tract and Stephen Atkinson's Fulling Mill tract
in relation to the city of Lancaster
Google map, Lancaster County, Pennsylvania

manner, so the record shows, he produced his own petition signed by his neighbors stating that he had been invited to build the fulling mill and dam and that the creek was too shallow and full of rocks for boats, but "to take off any Colour of Complaint" he would leave open a twenty foot wide passage way through which the fish could pass at all proper seasons. So ended the Assembly's involvement. (PA (8): 3: 2099)

Fresh from the fulling mill and back home, the women sewed the fabric into clothes and household items like tablecloths, sheets and towels. If Michael's family was similar to other self-sufficient farming families, they made most of their own furnishings. They would have made their own furniture from some of the "300 foot wall nots boarts" and the "150 foot oack boarts" that were inventoried, and they would have made their own shoes from the "5 Calfe Skins" he had.

For all the crops that Michael raised, his main interest appears to have been livestock, especially horses and cows. His estate had on 20 May, 1749 twenty-nine bovines and sixteen equines, that is twelve cows, five steer, five yearling calves, and seven two-yearling calves; one mare with three colts, three other colts, one bay mare, a grey 'bassing' mare, another bay mare with a two-yearling colt, a young stallion, two working horses, a bay horse, a three year old stallion colt. Only two of the horses were for field work and one had a saddle and bridle for riding. The estate also had twenty-five sheep and twelve hogs.

These animals required food. James Lemon, in *The Best Poor Man's Country* figures that thirteen acres of grain, thirteen acres of hay and fifteen acres of pasture could support 7 cows with calves, 1 steer, and 3 older calves. Five acres of grain, 6 acres of hay and 3 acres of pasture could support three or four horses and one yearling. Two acres of grain and mast could support 8 swine. Ten to twelve sheep could live on one-third acre grain and 1 acre pasture. *(Table 27: 153)* Michael Springle had considerably more livestock. To feed his livestock, he would have needed more than 60 acres in winter grain (spelt, barley, rye), perhaps twice as much, since his yield could have been as low as 10 bushels per acre. If we accept Lemon's figures, Michael might have produced one of the largest crops in Lancaster County. Even 10 years later, 1758-59, only the thirty-six wealthiest tax payers in Lancaster County each sowed more than thirty acres. *(Lemon 210)*

If we compare Michael's holdings to James Lemon's average holding's calculated from 61 inventories of Lancaster County deceased residents in 1750 we learn that Michael was 5 times wealthier. Lemon's average inventoried wealth was £153 whereas Michael's inventoried wealth showed a gross value of £755. *(Lemon, 88)* Comparing Michael's livestock holdings, alone, to the average livestock owned by Chester and Lancaster County residents in 1750 we learn that Michael had twice as many sheep (12.3 to 25), twice as many hogs (6-7 to 12), 3 times as many cattle (8.3 to 24), and 4 times as many horses (3.8 to 16) with 50%

versus 20% being young. In Connecticut between 1745 and 1747 a horse brought £26 local money or £4.11 Spanish Silver. Figures are not available for Lancaster or York counties.

Tax assessment in 1748 had not changed from the 1742 valuation rates. Michael's 500 acres would have been valued at £4 per hundred or £20. His horses and mares at £2 each or £16 for 4 adult horses and 4 adult mares. His cows at £1 each or £12 for 12 cows. His sheep at £1/8 or £3.1.10 for 25 sheep. His amount of winter grain is unknown. Adding what we have calculated comes to a valuation minimum of £51.1.10. The tax rate was 3 pence per pound valuation. Michael would have been assessed a minimum tax of 12s 8p. or approximately three times his tax when he left Conestoga Township.

Michael and Ann would have expected their children to help with the farm work and household chores. With four boys and ten girls, all the children of capable age would have been needed in the fields, with the animals, and doing the spinning as well. No wonder Michael needed five spinning wheels, one each for the four older girls and the big spinning wheel for Anna Margaret. Ann, as her father had called her in his will, preferred to be called Margaret as she signed her name on all documents associated with Michael's death. Existing evidence says that her full name was Anna Margaretha, a name she gave to daughter number four after naming daughter number two after her own mother, Anna Barbara. No evidence reinforces the idea that Michael had two wives - one named Ann and one named Margaret. No evidence exists, either, for the birth or baptismal dates of the children. To the best of all research, no Mennonite Meeting House named Lauck's existed in the 1740s. *(Ness, Lancaster Mennonite Historical Society)* Furthermore, Mennonites did and do not practice infant or child baptism and congregations kept no written records until much later.

A year after Michael's death his nine youngest children were still minors. By law they required court appointed guardians. Boys at age fourteen could choose their own guardian and girls could choose at age twelve, but none of Michael's children chose this option; they had no need to. If the order in which the minor children appeared in the Lancaster County Orphan's Court Docket 6 June 1749 appointing guardians George Myer and Michael Tanner is significant, their names and order of age were Michael, Margaret, Christian[a], Catherine, George, Eve, Henry, Mandoline and Mary.

To determine their ages, we must look at other documents. We do know that in 1762 when Michael's 500 acre Blunston tract was divided between Peter and Michael, Jr., Eva, although married, and Henry were still minors under the age of twenty-one so could not be parties to the indenture. We also know that Eva was younger than Henry. On October 22, 1764, Henry, with no wife mentioned, sold his interest to brother Peter, but on December 15, 1764, Henry, now with wife Mary, sold his interest to brother Michael. These two deeds indicate that Henry had reached the age of twenty-one in 1764 giving him a birth year of

1743 plus or minus one. Eva's release indentures to Peter and Michael, Jr., and to George, are all dated May 17, 1766. Although the deeds mention Eva's husband, Michael Miller, she was the primary releasor and therefore gives her a birth date of 1745. If the two year progression is accurate, Mandoline and Mary may have been twins born in 1747.

George was the youngest to have been a party to the November 15, 1762 indentures to Peter and Michael, Jr., indicating that he was then 21 or over so born about 1741. We have corroborating evidence of his birth year from his head stone in Saint Paul's Church Cemetery, also known as Wolf's Church Cemetery. Former transcriptions state that George was 63 years, 6 months old when he died on June 27, 1805. The years, months, and days are no longer legible, but calculation points to a December, 1741 birth before the 27th. *(findagrave)* The older children who were minors in 1749, Michael, Margaret, Christina, and Catharine were probably born in the same two year intervals, plus or minus one, giving them birth dates as follows: Catharine 1739, Christina 1737, Margaret 1735, Michael 1733.

Hier ruhen
die Gebine von
JOHAN GEORG
SPRENCKEL
Gestorben am June 27, 1805
remainder illegible

St Paul's Church Cemetery
York County, Pennsylvania
Courtesy of Margaret Sopp
December 1, 2010
Find A Grave Memorial # 62419704

The five oldest children were Peter, Elizabeth, Anna Barbara, Esther and Susannah. Their names appear on several deeds dealing with the distribution of Michael's land. Continuing backward in a two year progression, assuming all were single births, we come to Susannah who might have been either 17 or 18 in the spring of 1748 when father Michael died. She was definitely 18 by 6 June 1749 when guardians were assigned to the younger children since girls age 18 did not require guardians. Her birth year was probably 1731. Continuing in the two year progression we have Esther born 1729, Anna Barbara born 1727, Elizabeth born 1725, and Peter born 1723. All of these dates should be considered as plus or minus one. We do, however, have evidence that Peter was over 21 when his father died. According to the administrative accounts of Michael's estate, Peter was due £4.17. Pennsylvania German farm families expected boys and girls to work for their parents without pay until they were twenty-one years old or married. *(Long 2)* Knowing this we can be sure that Peter was over 21 in 1748, and, probably, the two oldest girls were over 21 and married.

Although we can calculate the children's approximate ages, no written record has yet been found to give us accurate birth and baptism dates for all. Of course, baptism dates for those raised Mennonites do not give us a birth age, anyway, since Mennonites practiced adult baptism. Their baptismal age varies with local congregations and other factors. During Michael's lifetime few organized churches existed on the west side of the Susquehanna River. Perhaps the first to be formed was the Lutheran Church on the Codorus, whose pastor was John Casper Stoever, but Michael was certainly not a Lutheran. His name was not among the twenty-four men who contributed to the purchase of the first record book of the Church in September 1733. *(Rooney email; Glatfelter I: 139-143; Schmucker 4-8; Schmauk 244-75)* Neither is Michael's name listed as a male member of the congregation between 1733 and 1743. *(Gibson 523)*

The first Brethren congregation organized in 1738. Their meeting place was near Black Rock, about 20 miles southwest of Michael and Margaret's and very near what would become the Maryland line. There are no baptismal records for this congregation from Michael or Margaret's lifetime. *(Gleim)* The First Reformed Church of York worshipped in a private house until Jacob Lischy arrived as its first pastor in 1744. Although Lischy's private record shows baptisms from 1743, none of Michael's children are included. *(Young; Humphrey, Ancestry.com)* Perhaps all of this tells us that it is more than likely that Michael and Margaret brought their family up as Mennonites who worshipped at home and believed in adult baptism. None of his nine minor children at the time of his death would have been baptized under normal circumstances and the older children might not have been baptized until they were about to marry. No Mennonite Meeting House existed on the west side of the Susquehanna until long after Michael's death when Bair's Meeting House was built. *(Gibson 694)*

Instead of attending a formal church service, Michael's children would have received their religious instruction at home. The children would have gathered around the family table to listened to and read from one of the family's two Bibles. Almost certainly the Bibles were in German and one of Michael's most valuable possessions. Each one, alone, was worth more than the "Bik Spinen Wheel" or the "Table." Together, they were worth twice as much as the "2 Chests." The Mennonites favorite Bible was published by Christopher Froschauer, a Swiss printer, in 1529, three years before the Luther Bible. Michael could have brought a copy of this Bible with him, or bought an imported Martin Luther translation. One of the Bibles might have been a Christopher Sauer Bible printed in German in Germantown, Pennsylvania near Philadelphia in 1742. Probably neither Bible had belonged to Margaret. One was not listed in father Rudy Miller's Inventory.

Along with his Bible, Michael's Inventory listed "Some other Books." These would also have been in German. Michael might have known enough English to communicate about business matters, but his preferred language was German as evidenced by the fact that his Will was written in German. He apparently preferred the role of a low key, but savvy Mennonite and made no effort to participate in political affairs. Likewise, he saw no reason to teach his children to write their names in English. Even fourteen and more years after his death, deeds dealing with the division of Michael's property show merely 'his mark' or 'her mark' beside the clerk's rendering of each sibling's name. An illegible scrawl with many, too many humps and bumps, wife Margaret's signature as Administratrix of Michael's estate shows her lack of familiarity with English, also. With no local school building, the children would have been home schooled and grown up speaking and reading German at home.

But what kind of home did they have? Michael's Inventory presents some clues. The house needed a room large enough to accommodate "4 spinnen Wheels" and the "Bik Spinen Wheel" also, and it needed to be warm enough in the winter for working the spinning wheels. A *Stube* or stove room, the main room of the house would qualify. In a traditional German early colonial house this room was heated by a closed jamb stove fed through the back side of the kitchen fireplace. The usual stove had five plates of iron - top, bottom, and three sides - while the fourth side was open to the fireplace in the kitchen. By 1734 several Pennsylvania furnaces made five-plate stoves. *(Other stoves were made of earthen ware, tiles, or plastered brick. Friesen 72; Seipt 367-70)*

Michael's stove room was undoubtedly multipurpose as was common before 1750. Besides being a spinning room, it could be used as a parlor, dining room, family living room, and even a sleeping room. As houses grew larger, so did stoves. Peter Sprenkle, William's son, bequeathed to his wife in 1813 his ten plate stove and pipe that he had installed in his new dwelling house. *(Will of Peter Sprenkle, 1813. York County Archives)*

Michael's house had either two or three other rooms on the main floor. The traditional modest German home of the time had a three room floor plan. Behind the *Stube* would have been the *Kammer*, or chamber. The stove could have been placed so that it formed part of the wall between the two rooms as it was in the Herr house in Conestoga Township. *(Friesen 64)* The *Kammer* would have contained the chests listed in Michael's inventory and one or two of the "2 beds" with two of the "3 bett Steads." In German terms, it took a bed or flat mattress made of linen filled straw and a bedstead to make a complete bed. Bed cord was used to support the mattress. *(Websters Unabridged 1.a.; Wills of George and Peter Sprenkle, York County Archives)* Michael would have kept his bonds, notes and ready cash in one of the chests along with "his Cloth" either clothes or negotiable linen. Note that Michael's Cloth was the single most valuable household item at £3.10.0. It was common practice among the Germans to keep a fair amount of cash on hand and Michael had £48.8.0. at home when he died. Christian Herr's 1750 inventory from Conestoga Township showed that he had £130 on hand - half of his total monetary value - when he died. (Friesen 59) Michael, Margaret and the youngest children would have slept in the *kammer*.

Jamb or five-plate iron stove c. 1766
Mary Ann Furnace, Manheim Township,
York County, Pennsylvania
Courtesy Falk 22
from Winterthur Museum

The third room would have been the *Kuche* or kitchen. Entrance to a typical three room house was through the kitchen which had a fireplace and staircase to a loft or attic level. All of Michael's inventoried cooking utensils, "an Iron pott & 3 Pans, Iron Ledles & ? fork, a Cooper Kettle," and other utensils not inventoried would have been in the *Kuche*, or kitchen. Usually the fireplace had a raised hearth which was more suitable to small fires and much safer than floor level fires. Boiled foods and hearth baking in a Dutch oven were most common. Certainly Margaret and the girls needed a kitchen table and a kitchen cupboard, but those items were not usually inventoried. Kitchens were sparsely furnished.

If Michael had a fourth room on the first floor, as the Christian Herr house in Conestoga had, it would have been a Kammerli or combined pantry and workroom behind the kitchen. (Friesen 77) Four room houses were more square, while three room house were rectangular. The Herr four room house measured about 30 by 38 feet.

Bertolet-Herbein house
c. 1737-1750
Entry-kitchen house
and floor plan.

Originally Oley Township, Berks County, since moved to Danial Boone Homestead, Berks County, Pennsylvania

Courtesy Falk, 20-21 From Library of Congress, Prints and Photographs, HABS, HABS-PA, 6-LIMKI.V.5

Whether three or four rooms, Michael's house would have had an unheated loft or attic where the older children slept, some on one or two of the "3 bett Steads" on straw filled linen mattresses supported by bed cord. The attic would also have been used for storage, especially for grain before taking it to the grist mill.

Under the house there might have been a cellar or springhouse with a separate outside entrance. Michael's inventory lists "6 Casks big and Little" which would have stored cider, vinegar, cabbages, and other food stuffs that needed to be kept cool. Other food that simply needed to be kept cool, but protected from freezing would be stored in a cellar.

Since Michael Springle's Inventory does not include a description of his dwelling house we can only wonder if his house was built of logs or stone? The earliest extant stone house in Lancaster County is the Christian Herr house. That house dates from 1719, several years before Michael built his house, and is located on the east side of the Susquehanna River where it was easier and safer to live. Built by Christian Herr and restored in the 1970s, the house was renamed for Herr's father, Hans Herr, and stands today as a museum. (Friesen 101-09)

Christian and Anna Herr's stone house, 1719
Renamed The Hans Herr House
Lancaster, Pennsylvania
Friesen, 60

Herr House First floor plan
Falk 68 from Schiffer 376

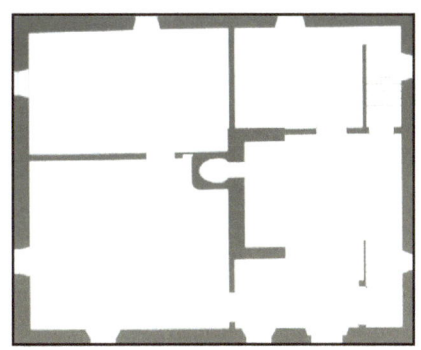

By 1798, Michael's Blunston tract contained three stone houses. One was on the eastern 200 acre portion that went to Michael, Jr., but in 1798 belonged to Christian Harnish. Measuring 40 by 30 feet, that house had two stories, with 20 windows containing 300 panes of glass. The two other stone houses were on the western 300 acre portion that went to son Peter and later to Peter's sons Peter, Jr., Daniel and Michael. Daniel had a one story stone house, 30 by 28 with 3 windows containing 36 panes of glass. Michael, was in the process of selling his one story stone house to Christian Huber. That house was 26 by 24 and had 5 windows with 70 panes of glass. There was also one wood house on the Blunston tract, but the 1798 Direct Tax entry describing the house does not make it clear whether it was only a spring house or a dwelling house over a spring house. It measured only 23 by 22 and had 2 windows with 6 panes of glass each. *(United States Direct Tax of 1798)* How assuring it would be to know that Michael Springle had built the largest of the stone houses, but we have no evidence. All we can say based upon facts is that the location of the large stone house is favorable in that friend George Myer's tract adjoined on the east and on the west there was a wagon trail that in 1758 became the road to Manheim Township and the Maryland line; and that in 1802 Peter, Jr. bought back that 200 acres and stone house after it had been out of the family for thirty-two years. *(Hively, Springettsbury Map; York Deed 2-Q-475)*

Michael was more than twice as wealthy when he died in 1748 than Christian Herr was when he died in 1750. Considered to be "one of the wealthiest members of the Mennonite community" Herr's Inventory prior to the final settlement of his accounts valued his estate at £352.15.0. *(Friesen 59, 93)* Michael's Inventory valued his estate at £716.3.4 after administration of his accounts. Further, Christian was a minister holding meetings in his house, but had "One Bible," whereas Michael had "2 Bibles." Both had sundry or other Books. Herr had no spinning wheels, but he had "Two Stills," a "Cider Press," and 12 Hogsheads presumably for aging cider. Both men raised hemp, but Herr's "Forty One Pound" was valued at £1.15.0 whereas Michael's fresh hemp was valued at £40.0.0. Another difference came in the amount of book debt, bonds, and notes due to each of them. Herr had only £25 of "Book Debt," whereas Michael was a veritable bank. He had £64.8.0 out on loan. The biggest difference of all was in the amount of livestock each man had. Herr had only "One Cow and Haifer." Michael, as pointed out earlier had twenty-five sheep, twelve hogs, twelve calves, twelve cows, four mares, seven colts, three horses, two stallions.

Michael's livestock and other farm items could be another clue to the location of his house. He certainly would have wanted a barn for his animals in the winter and cover for his "Plantation wagon" and his "big wagon," as well as his "two old Plows and Harrow." He needed a place to store his "Fresh Hemp," his "150 foot oack boarts," his "300 foot wall nots boarts," his "10 bushel of Flax Seed," and his chains and other tools. Usually barns were located in the leeward direction from the house, on the other side of the garden and barnyard. Many barns were built on level sites, not banked. *(Long 314-17)* Michael's hogs were probably kept in the barn, as were the chickens, ducks, and geese that he might have had but would not have been inventoried. The yearling colts and calves, with their parents, the work horses, and other horses and cows would keep the barn warm.

Pennsylvania winters could be brutal. March, 1741 saw snow in Lancaster County more than three feet deep and cattle dying for lack of fodder. Back settlers were reported suffering for want of bread and many families had little to eat but the carcasses of dead deer. *(The Pennsylvania Gazette, April 9, 1741)* Winters from 1742 through 1746 were more moderate, but in 1747 the Delaware River was frozen up between December 23 and February 24. January and February 1748 likewise experienced severe weather with the Delaware full of ice. *("Pennsylvania Weather Records," 111-112; Gelber 32)* Other winters were more mild so that the average annual temperature in Philadelphia 1738-1748 was 55.28 degrees, plenty warm enough for livestock to remain out-of-doors. However, that figure belies the average January temperature 1748-1749 of 33.5 degrees. The average annual winter temperature at Philadelphia 1738-1748 (with figures for 9 of the 11 years) was 34.9 degrees with the average winter temperature in 1741 at a cold 30 degrees. *(Purvis, Tables 1.3 - 1.6)*

The barn on the 200 acres that had gone to Michael, Jr. was of comparatively modest size for as many animals as Michael Springle owned. Measuring 50 by 25 feet, the barn was made of wood, but its height and number of levels were not recorded. Between 1772 and 1802, that tract with house and barn belonged to others. In 1798 there were three barns on the 300 acres that went to Peter. Grandson Daniel owned a good size, stone barn 60 by 36 feet. Although 336 square feet smaller than the stone barn on the Herr property in 1798, it was nevertheless in the top twenty percent of all barns if Falk's calculations for Coventry Township, Chester County are representative for south central Pennsylvania. *(Falk 49)* Grandson Michael also owned a large stone barn measuring 60 by 30 feet. He was in the process of selling. Grandson Peter, Jr. owned the third barn. It was made of logs and not considered of sufficient value to measure. His investment was in the saw, hemp and oil mills he had taken over after father Peter died. Michael Springle's 1746 warrant tract of 238 acres is not included for consideration as a location for his home or barn. He warranted it only two years before he died. *(United States Direct Tax of 1798)*

Although we have an incomplete picture of Michael's farmstead, by knowing the recurring pattern in farmstead arrangement, we can add to the picture from another reliable source, Amos Long and his research of *The Pennsylvania German Family Farm*. Long points out the importance of a convenient access to a road and surrounding fields in selecting a site for the house, barn, and out buildings. Michael apparently assumed that his tract lay adjacent to the old Indian trail, as did the surveyors who laid out the Monocacy Road along the same trail, but upon Cookson's survey of Michael's land, his northern line lay about a half mile south of the road. Michael did not apply for a warrant for the 454 acres that intervened. He probably already had access along a trail that bisected his own 500 acres and ran north-south between the old Indian trail and a trail that in 1758 became the road between York and the Maryland line. His homestead was located on one side or the other of this north-south track that also took him directly to where his meadows would have been along Codorus Creek. As Long points out, "the best permanent meadows were located on the two sides of a land depression with a small stream flowing through at the lowest level." *(Long 23; Hively, Springettsbury Map)*

Nearly all German farmsteads had a garden, a yard, and an orchard for as one early writer observed, the Germans "lived more on vegetables than any other people, and make gardens accordingly." The kitchen back door usually led to the garden which was about a half acre in size on the warm side of the house, surrounded by a secure fence to keep animals out. There, the women raised cabbage, onions, turnips, all sorts of vegetables that stored easily. Nearby, maybe bordering the garden, would have been the orchard, mainly apples, on the first field cleared. *(Long 37)*

Michael's out buildings would have included a spring house, if not under the main house. All neighboring farms in the 1798 Direct Tax records included a spring house. A vital part of the farmstead, the spring house would have been close enough to the farm house to easily get water to the kitchen. Long points out how important a springhouse was during the hot Pennsylvania summers for farmers like Michael who had a large number of cattle. The cow's milk could be kept cool and drinking water could be protected from contamination. Other foodstuffs could be kept cool, as well. *(Long 106)*

The only other building we can assuredly say Michael had on his farmstead was an outdoor privy. Located fairly close to the house so it could be reached quickly and easily, sometimes the privy was attached to a wash house, therefore close to a water source. *(Long 229-43)* Farms with additional out buildings such as summer kitchen, bake oven, smoke house, even chicken house, pig pen, sheepfold, and so on, were located closer to Philadelphia, or date from the later colonial period.

An Unexpected Death

Unexpectedly, Michael died in the spring of 1748, cause unknown. His exact date of death has never been discovered. On Monday, June 6, 1748, wife Margaret, neighbor George Myer, and friend Michael Tanner appeared in the town of Lancaster, at the Court House, to register Michael's Will and sign an administration bond. Myer, a witness to the Will, owned the tract adjoining Michael's to the east. Tanner, the recognized community leader, lived four miles east adjoining York Town. The other witness, Michael Woolrich, probably Wallick, appeared in court four days later on June 10. He owned the tract just east of Tanner. Perhaps Margaret had a copy of Michael's Will, written in German, with her, but she did not have an English translation as was and still is required by law for recording. Thomas Cookson, the Deputy Surveyor and Deputy Register of Wills signed a terse and unclear entry, now in Will Book A-1, page 154 on this matter and has confused researchers ever since. Abstractors have rephrased Cookson's words and left differing impressions, but there is no doubt that the will was not recorded. The entry as it now reads says, "The Last Will and Testament of Michael Sprinkle Deced being wrote in the German Language could not be entered But thereon is endorsed as Follows Vizt." Then follows the record for George Mayor [sic Myer], having taken the oath that he was present and saw and heard Michael Springle sign his Will. That entry is dated 6th June 1748 and signed by Tho Cookson, DR. Next follows the same record for Michael Woolrich [sic.Wallick], but signed by George Swope and dated June the 10th day 1748. These entries were made in the Will Book on July 25.

Will Book Entry for Michael Sprinkle, Deceased
Lancaster County Will Book A-1-154

The fact that the Will was not presented in translation is very strange, indeed, because both Tanner and Myer were supposedly bilingual and Tanner, at least, would have known that a translation was required. Nevertheless, following probate procedure of the time, Letters of Administration were granted to Margaret Springle as Administratrix with Michael Tanner and George Myer as joint executors. All three were held in bond for one thousand pounds should an inventory of Michael's "Goods & Chattles Rights & Credits" not be completed by the sixth day of June, 1749 and exhibited at the Register's office in Lancaster by the sixth day of July 1749. *(Michael Springle Estate Papers, LancasterHistory.org)* Thus, they had one year to complete the inventory of Michael's estate, collect all credits, and settle all debts.

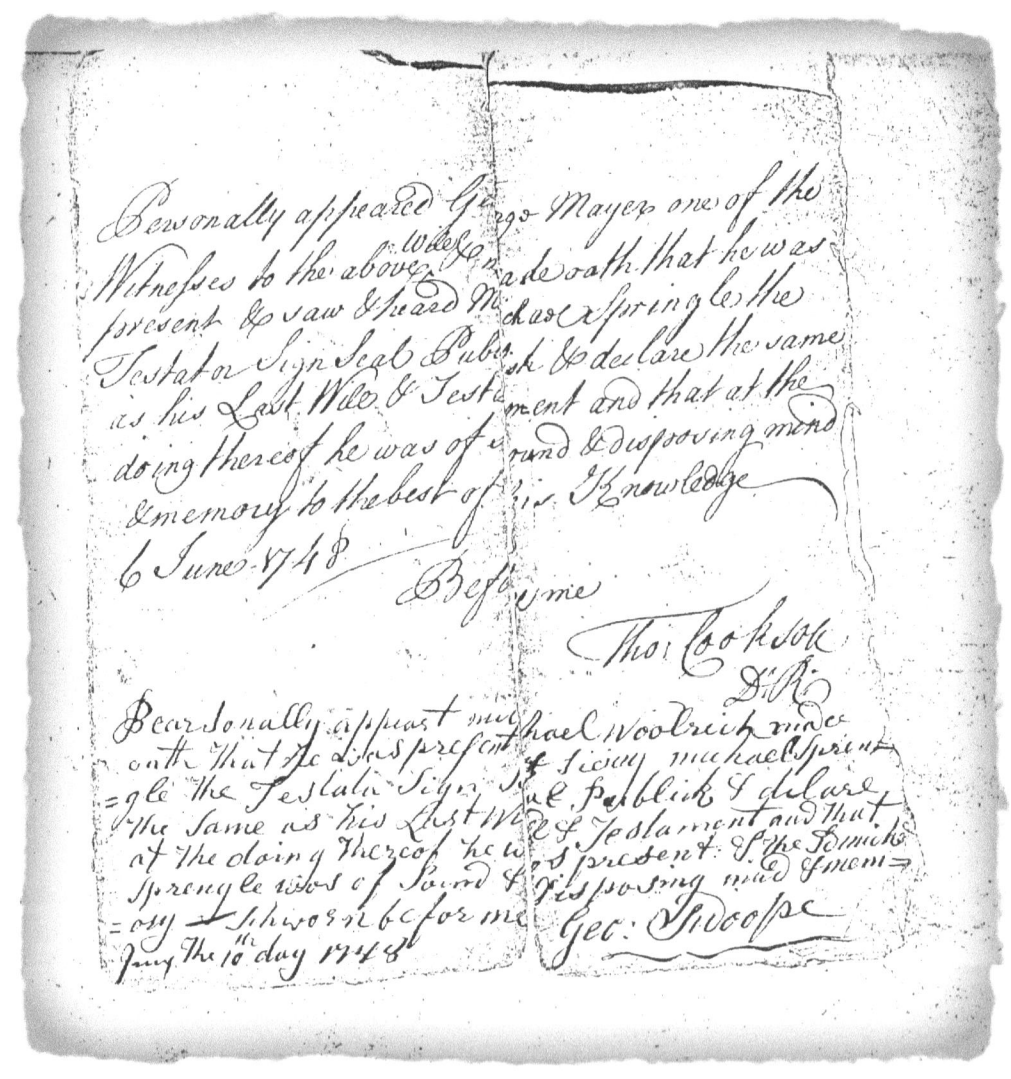

Surviving Fragment of Michael Springle's Will
Lancaster County Archives

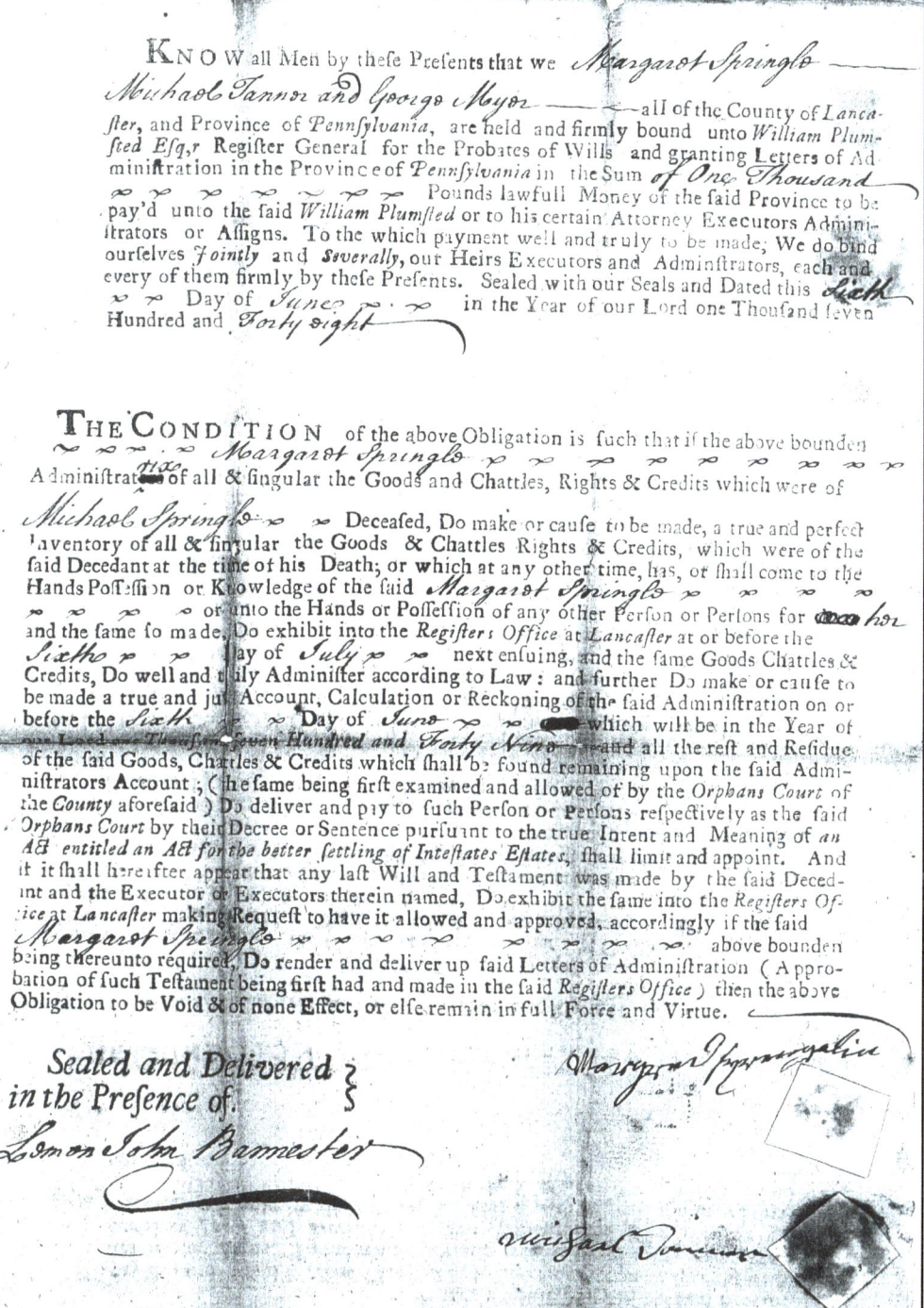

KNOW all Men by these Presents that we Margaret Springle Michael Tanner and George Meyer all of the County of Lancaster, and Province of Pennsylvania, are held and firmly bound unto William Plumsted Esq,r Register General for the Probates of Wills and granting Letters of Administration in the Province of Pennsylvania in the Sum of One Thousand Pounds lawfull Money of the said Province to be pay'd unto the said William Plumsted or to his certain Attorney Executors Administrators or Assigns. To the which payment well and truly to be made, We do bind ourselves Jointly and Severally, our Heirs Executors and Administrators, each and every of them firmly by these Presents. Sealed with our Seals and Dated this Sixth Day of June in the Year of our Lord one Thousand seven Hundred and Forty eight

THE CONDITION of the above Obligation is such that if the above bounden Margaret Springle Administratrix of all & singular the Goods and Chattles, Rights & Credits which were of Michael Springle Deceased, Do make or cause to be made, a true and perfect Inventory of all & singular the Goods & Chattles Rights & Credits, which were of the said Decedant at the time of his Death; or which at any other time, has, or shall come to the Hands Possession or Knowledge of the said Margaret Springle or unto the Hands or Possession of any other Person or Persons for her and the same so made, Do exhibit into the Registers Office at Lancaster at or before the Sixth Day of July next ensuing, and the same Goods Chattles & Credits, Do well and truly Administer according to Law: and further Do make or cause to be made a true and just Account, Calculation or Reckoning of the said Administration on or before the Sixth Day of June which will be in the Year of our Lord one Thousand Seven Hundred and Forty Nine and all the rest and Residue of the said Goods, Chattles & Credits which shall be found remaining upon the said Administrators Account; (the same being first examined and allowed of by the Orphans Court of the County aforesaid) Do deliver and pay to such Person or Persons respectively as the said Orphans Court by their Decree or Sentence pursuant to the true Intent and Meaning of an Act entitled an Act for the better settling of Intestates Estates, shall limit and appoint. And if it shall hereafter appear that any last Will and Testament was made by the said Decedent and the Executor or Executors therein named, Do exhibit the same into the Registers Office at Lancaster making Request to have it allowed and approved, accordingly if the said Margaret Springle above bounden being thereunto required, Do render and deliver up said Letters of Administration (Approbation of such Testament being first had and made in the said Registers Office) then the above Obligation to be Void & of none Effect, or else remain in full Force and Virtue.

Sealed and Delivered in the Presence of.

Simon John Bannester

Administrators' Bond Michael Springle
LancasterHistory.org

To our benefit, Michael Tanner and George Myer, with the additional help of Samuel Bechtel, a Mennonite who lived near Hanover in Manheim (Heidelberg 1750) Township prepared "an Inventory of all the Estates Chattles & Cattles of Michael Sprengle" dated the 20th day of May, 1749. Margaret completed her account of the payments and disbursements of £38.1.4 owed by Michael's estate and that was exhibited, as required, at the Register's office in Lancaster and dated June 6, 1749. The Inventory was submitted at the same time, but the recording date was not written on the paper.

On the same day, the Orphans Court appointed George Myer and Michael Tanner "Guardians over Michael, Margaret, Christian[a], Catherine, George, Eve, Henry Mandoline and Mary Springle, orphan children of Michael Springle, decd." Many researchers and abstractors, have been confused by this phrasing, thinking that the children named were Michael's entire family. Later deeds, however, prove that Michael also had five children of legal age when he died: Peter, Elizabeth, Anna Barbara, Esther, Susannah.

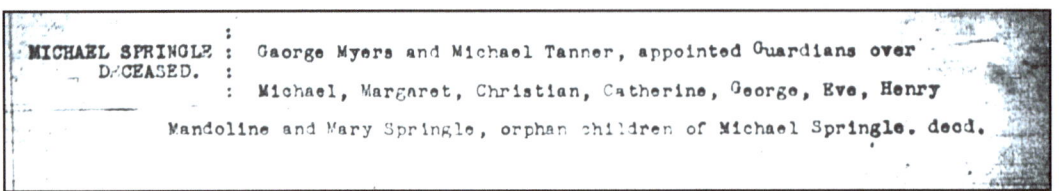

Guardianship of Michael Springle's Minor Children
Lancaster County Archives. Orphan's Court Docket, 6 June 1749: 53
Original does not exist, only this transcript

Evidence from George's grave marker, already discussed, indicates that George would have turned seven four days before June 6, 1748 when his mother was appointed administratrix of his father's estate, so was six when Michael died. Other evidence from later deeds indicates that Henry was four going on five when Michael died and that Eva was three nearing four. Mandoline and Mary were two or younger. Going in the ascending direction from George with the children's ages when father Michael died and taking into account the difference between Michael's month of death and the child's month of birth, we have Catherine, 8-9; Christina, 10-11, Margaret 12-13, Michael, Jr. 14-15, Susannah, 17-18, Esther 19-20, Anna Barbara, 21-22, Elizabeth 23-24, Peter, 25-26. Margaret was thus left to raise nine children under sixteen years of age, but she did have the significant help of five children over sixteen, although the two oldest girls may already have been married.

Where Michael was buried is unknown. The administration of his accounts lists only creditors by name except for Michael the Smith. We have not found a record of Michael belonging to the Kreutz Creek Union (Lutheran and Reformed) Church in existence from the mid 1740s, nor does his name appear in Stoever's or later records of the Lutheran

An Inventory of all the Estates Chattles & Cattles &
of Michael Sprengle of Manchester Township
in the County of Lancaster Deceased Made by
Michael Palmer George Myer & Samuel Becktle
on the 20th day of may in the year Annoy Doni 1748

		£	s	d
Firstly	To a Lantern	0	5	0
	To a Chest	0	15	0
	To a Bik Spinen Wheel	0	7	0
	To an iron pott & 3 Pans	0	16	0
	To Iron Ledles & Flesh fork	0	12	0
	To a Cooper Ketle	2	0	0
	To Putter whare	2	12	0
	To 2 Chests	1	1	0
	To 4 Spinen Wheels	0	5	0
	To 10 Sikles	0	14	0
	To 10 bushel of Flax Seed	1	0	0
	To 5 Calfe Skins	0	8	0
	To 3 bett Steads	0	4	0
	To 15 old Sack	1	5	0
	To Boslen Tools	0	0	0
	To a pott Chain	0	6	0
	To a halter Chain	0	4	0
	To 2 Sice	0	4	0
	To old Iron	0	3	0
	To a haoye hows Shouffe furk & Toongrieb	1	5	0
	To 11 bees hife with the bees	2	15	0
	To a Grain Stone	0	12	0
	To 4 Rittles	0	2	0
	To 4 pine Cooper whare	0	8	0
	To 4 tops 1 Chorn & woolen funnel	0	18	0
	To 6 Casks big & Little	0	15	0
	To a Stone Chok	0	1	0
	To Earthen whare	0	5	0
	To 300 foot wallnots boarts	1	0	0
	To 100 foot oack boarts	0	7	0

Michael Sprenckle/Sprengle Estate Inventory, page 1
LancasterHistory.org

		L	s	d
To 2 wooll Cards		0	2	0
To 6 breds		0	10	0
To 5 Shingle meals		0	15	0
To a Table		0	8	0
To 2 Bibles		2	0	0
To Som other Books		0	15	0
To 2 beds		3	0	0
To his Cloth		3	10	0
To 25 Sheep		6	0	0
To 12 hogs		2	0	0
To 5 yearling Calfes		2	10	0
To 7 two yearling		7	0	0
To 5 Steers		6	5	0
To 12 Cows		27	0	0
To a mare with three Colts		7	0	0
To 3 yealing Colts		5	0	0
To a bay mare		7	0	0
To a Gray breeding mare with Sadle & bridle		12	0	0
To a bay mare & a 2 yearling Colt		4	0	0
To young Stallion		10	0	0
To 2 working Horses		8	10	0
To a bay Horse		6	0	0
To a big wagon		14	0	0
To a 3 yearling Stalion Colt		1	10	0
To a Plandation wagon		4	0	0
To two old Plows and Harrow		1	10	0
To Gears & Collars		1	5	0
To the Lower improfement		5	0	0
To book Debt		14	9	0
To a bond		6	0	0
To a note		9	3	4
To a note		3		4
To a note		9	3	4
To a bond & note		23	0	0
To Ready Cash		48	8	0
To Drest Hemp		40	0	0

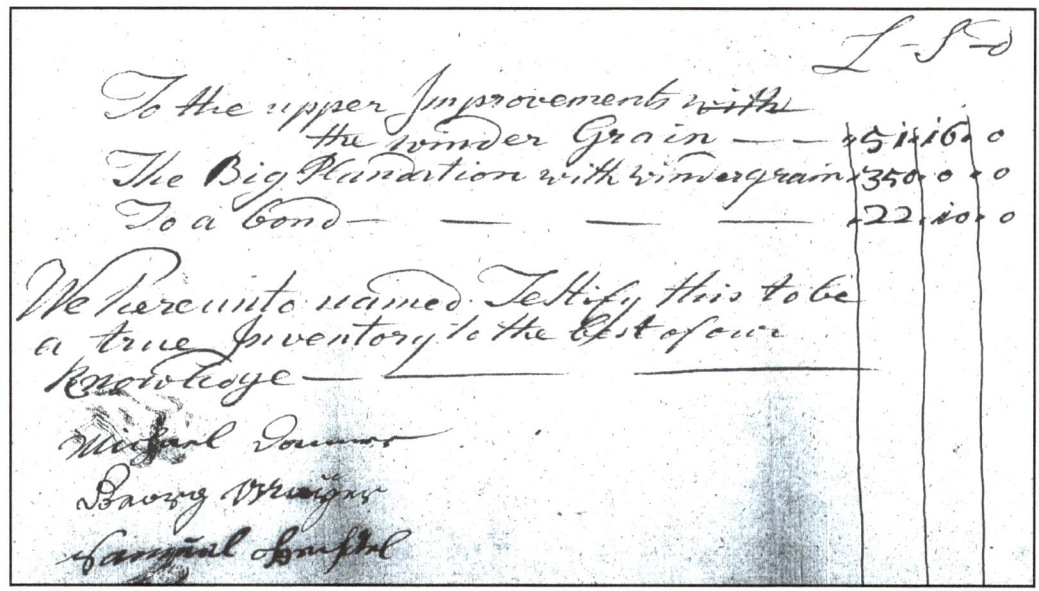

Michael Sprenckle/Sprengle Estate Inventory, page 3
LancasterHistory.org

Church on the Codorus, now Christ Evangelical Lutheran Church, records beginning 1733, nor records of Jacob Lischy, Pastor of the Reformed Church, records beginning 1744. Significantly, both Michael Tanner and Samuel Bechtel were Mennonites. Bechtel owned land in Digges' Choice which his sons Christian and Martin inherited when their father died in 1758. *(Bankert: Tract 1a-e: 1-3)* An old headstone for Samuel Bechtel is in Bairs Meeting House Cemetery near Hanover, but it was placed there years after his death. The official warrant for the Meeting House land was dated 1774. Tanner/Danner died in 1781; a newer headstone for him is in the same cemetery. Michael Springle was probably buried on his own farm, in a family plot near the house or in the highest spot, under trees, in one of the fields. *(Gibson 694-5)*

Whether Michael really had a Will or not is a moot point. The record of Margaret's administration of Michael's accounts initialed by Thomas Cookson, clearly states that the balance is to be distributed according to the directions in the Will. In practice, his land was ultimately distributed similarly to intestacy law: one-third to the widow and all the residue, by equal portions to and among the children. *(PSL: 2 St.L.199 Ch. 135)* What is different in Michael's case is that for fourteen years following Michael's death his land remained intact as it was originally. It was home for the children and for Margaret until she remarried. Peter and Michael, Jr. even settled on their own respective portions before legally separating the 500 acre Blunston tract. There may be a legal explanation for this; Michael had never been naturalized.

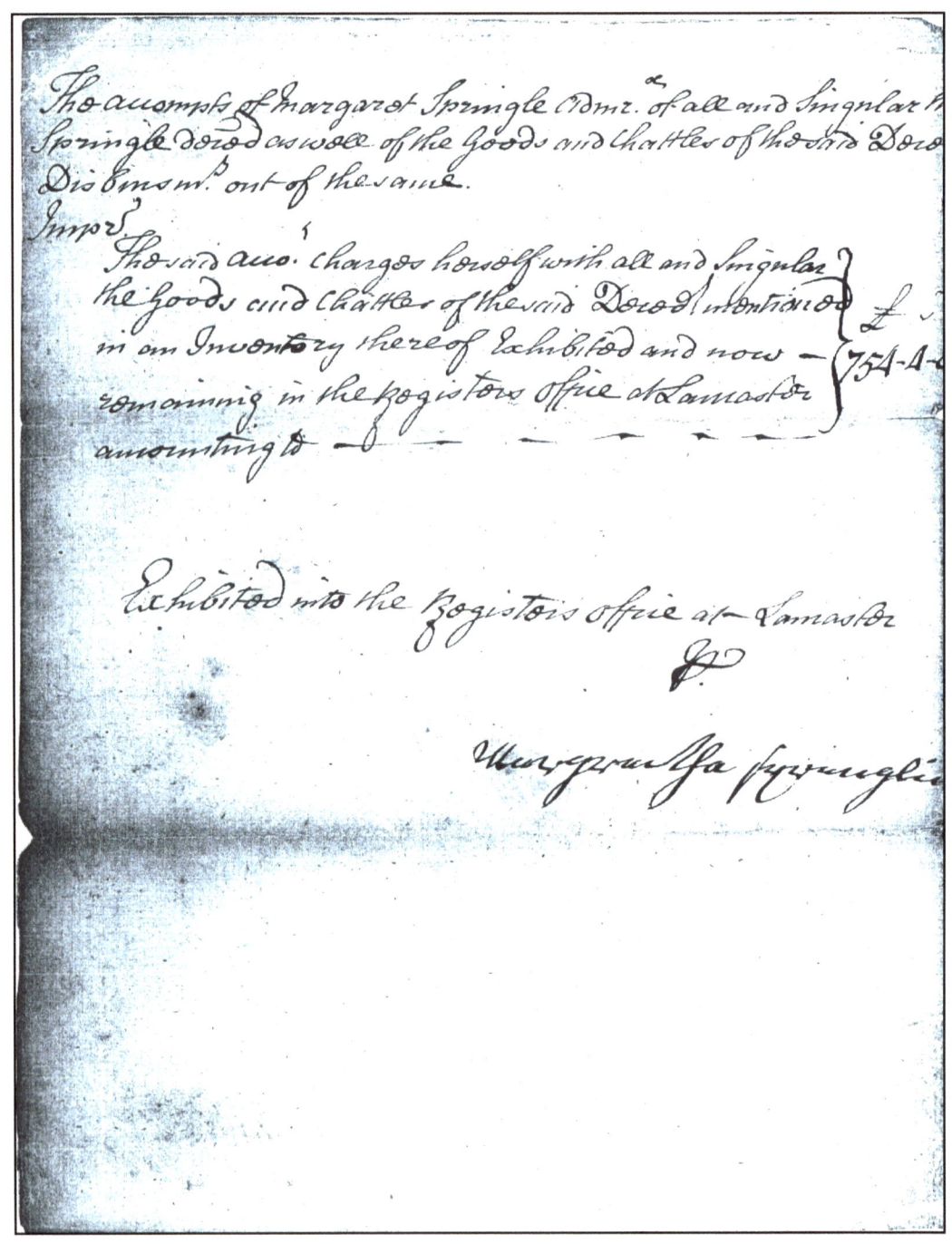

Administrative Accounts Michael Springle
6th June 1749
Left side

To Goods and Chattles Rights and Credits which were of Michal dec.d which came to the hands of the said Accn.t as of her paym.t &

Item The said Accn.t prays an allowance of her paym.ts and Disbursm.ts as follows

	£ s d
To p.d Matthew Atkinson as p receipt	2-16-8
To p.d Mark Hans	0-2-3
To p.d Geo: Swope	0-15-0
To p.d Geo: Inyers 4. To p.d Anthony Noble 0	4-6-0
To p.d Peter Springle	4-0-0
To p.d John Road	2-11-2
To p.d Christian Crawl	0-2-6
To p.d Register for Letters admon.r	1-5-0
To p.d Christian Bixler 7. To Martin Miller 15	1-2-0
To p.d Peter Sprinkler 17. To John Diordoff 3	1-0-0
To p.d Jacob Ross 1-12. To Bartho: Inorl 7-6	1-19-6
To p.d Jacob Miller 1-3. To Michael Dammer 2-6	0-3-9
To p.d Jacob Dammer 3-0 To Geo: Inyer 2-6	0-5-6
To p.d Michael Dammer 14-10. To Barbara Shrisser 2-7	0-17-5
To p.d Geo: Swope 2. To John Nicholas m.ag 1	0-3-0
To p.d Jacob Boin 1-9. To Ulrich Rudysiller 8-9	1-17-6
To Christian Bixler 18. To Michael the Smith 7-6	1-5-6
To Grospon in Maryland	0-9-0
Drawing Admon Acco Copy & 2 Notes	0-10-6
Allow'd Adm.rx for Extraordinary trouble & Expences	12-0-0
	38-1-4
Balance remaining in the Adm.rs hands to be distributed according to the directions of the Will	716-3-4
	754-4-8

Administrative Accounts Michael Springle
6th June 1749
Right side

Naturalization and inheritance were bound together. Aliens could not convey their land to others and their children could not inherit. To the best of our knowledge, Michael had never availed himself of the opportunity of any one of the several special laws to make his declaration of fidelity, to certify his Christian belief, and to take and affirm the abjuration oath before a judge of the supreme court. The law passed February 3, 1742-43, to which so many researchers refer as granting blanket naturalization, still required the preceding three steps. However, in 1759, the assembly addressed the issue of persons who had owned land and died unnaturalized. Henceforth and retroactively, all land conveyed by unnaturalized persons by deed, by will, or according to intestate law was to be considered as legal as that of natural born citizens. *(PSL 5 St.L. 443 Ch. 445)* Although repealed by the King in Council a year later, provincials paid no attention. Unnaturalized persons had been conveying and willing land in Pennsylvania during the entire colonial era and no one took legal action against them. *(PSL 5 St.L. 669 Appendix 23, Sec. 1, No. 8)* Yet, to be strictly legal, in 1778 the general assembly of the Commonwealth of Pennsylvania passed a law making valid the title of lands held under persons born out of the allegiance of the Crown of Great Britain and who had died not having been naturalized. *(PSL 9 St.L. 258 Ch. 803)*

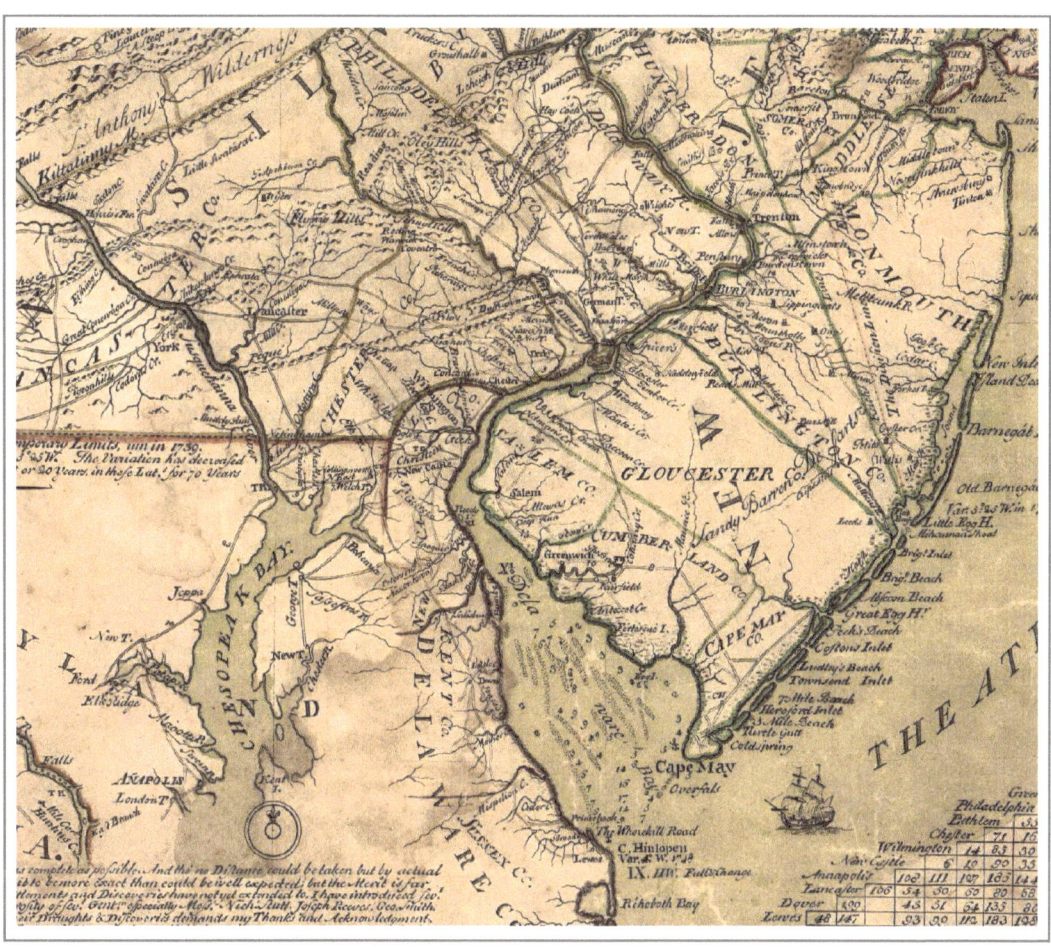

Portion of a Map of Pensilvania [sic], etc. by Lewis Evans, 1749.
This may be the first map of Pennsylvania published in the American colonies.
Image from the Library of Congress where a version in German also exists.
Courtesy mapsofpa.com

Melish-Whiteside Map of W. Manchester Township, York County 1818
Note Springles M.
Pennsylvania State Archives

3 Michael Springle's Plantation Lands

Springetsbury Manor Resurvey

Answering the question of what happened to Michael Springle's plantation lands is as interesting as answering questions about Michael's life. Sixty years after his death, the ownership of his land became the model in a court case for a class of settlers claiming title under licenses granted by Samuel Blunston. Discussing the course of events that led to this situation, and the results, is the main focus of this section.

Six years after Michael Springle's death, the family had his Blunston tract resurveyed and divided between Peter and Michael, Jr. Presumably, George Stevenson, then deputy surveyor for York County, conducted the survey, although he did not sign his name. The date, June 15, 1754, however, was recorded on the survey. Remembering that Michael, Jr. had been fourteen or fifteen when his father died in 1748, the survey and date is significant evidence that Michael, Jr. had turned twenty-one and was eligible to inherit land in his own name. The survey gave Peter 372 acres of the western portion and Michael, Jr. the eastern 190 acres making the original tract now 562 acres rather than 500 acres. No deed was drawn and filed and later surveys changed the number of acres for each, but the older boys now had their own farms, but not the title. *(York Survey 9480, Hively, Springettsbury 75)* For eight years they carried on life as normal. Their widowed mother, Margaret, had married Henry Everhart and settled on the 1746 warrant tract with the youngest children. George still lived with her. Henry may have been living with either Peter or Michael, Jr. and working for them as later deeds may show.

Near the end of May, 1762 the family's comfortable farming life was shaken by the news that Springetsbury Manor was to be resurveyed. *(Copied Survey D-113-179-80; Bair 197-98)* Many York County residents had never heard of Springetsbury Manor and did not know where it was located. They perhaps knew that some patents had been written as of the Manor of Maske and required an annual quitrent, but that provision had never been enforced. Peter and Michael, Jr. undoubtedly knew that their father had acquired his land on a Blunston license, but the license certainly did not include any comment about Springetsbury Manor.

Not sure what the resurvey would mean for them, Peter and Michael, Jr. learned that the manor would now extend far enough west to include their land. Instead of running mainly north and south as originally laid out, and excluding their tract, the resurvey would run east and west to include York Town and all the tracts for which Thomas Penn had signed licenses in 1736. Among those fifty-two, the most westerly was Christian Esther's [Oyster, Eyster] land, two property's west of theirs. *(Blunston License Book; Hively, Springettsbury Map)*

Researchers give many reasons for the resurvey of Springetsbury Manor. Governor James Hamilton's warrant, itself, states several reasons: (1) the original survey, by some accident was lost or mislaid; (2) although many tracts within the manor have been surveyed and patented, many remained to be patented; (3) to ascertain the bounds and lines of the manor with certainty; (4) to map and described carefully and distinctly the Town of York; and (5) to also map and describe carefully the tracts which have already been granted or surveyed for the settlers or any others by virtue of a warrant.

Pennsylvania ss.

By the Proprietaries

Whereas by Warrant under the hand & Seal of our late Honoured Father William Penn Esquire dated the first day of September 1700 Edward Pennington then Surveyor General of the said Province was required in pursuance of the primitive regulation for laying out Lands in the said Province to survey or cause to be surveyed to the proper use of our said Father and his Heirs the proportion of Five hundred Acres for every Township consisting of Five thousand acres that should be surveyed in the said Province and generally one tenth part of all the Lands laid out and to be laid out within the same. And Whereas the like Warrants from our Father and ourselves have been issued to every succeeding Surveyor General of this Province since that time, but notwithstanding no such Warrants and Orders to his and our Surveyor Generals from time to time the Tracts and Quantities of Land surveyed under the same fell greatly short of the Complement and proportion which ought to have been Surveyed & Returned for his and our use. And therefore by the order and Direction of the then Commissioners of Property and in virtue of the General Warrant aforesaid to the then Surveyor General, there was Surveyed for our use on the nineteenth and twentieth days of June 1722 a certain Tract of Land situate on the West side of the River Susquehannah, then in the County of Chester afterwards Lancaster & now within our County of York containing about Twenty Thousand Acres, called and now well known by the name of the Manor of Springetsbury. And Whereas sundry Germans & others afterwards seated themselves by our leave on divers parts of the said Manor but by reason of some Claim made to those Lands by the Indians of the Five Nations (which they afterwards released to us by their Deed of the 11 day of October 1736) the Confirmances of the parts so seated in the said Manor were for some time delayed. And Whereas upon our obtaining the said Release from the said Indians we did give each to of the persons so as aforesaid settled on our said Manor respectively our Licence or Certificate bearing date the 30 day of October in the Year last aforesaid thereby promising that we would order a patent to be drawn to each of them for their respective Settlements and Plantations in the said Manor as soon as Surveyed making in the whole by Computation 12,000 Acres or thereabouts, as in and by a Record & particular List of Such

Springetsbury Manor Warrant to Resurvey, 21 May 1762, page 1
Original Loose Survey, D-113-179-80, Pennsylvania State Archives

such Licences or Grants remaining in our Land Office more fully appear And Whereas the Survey of our said Manor is by some Accident lost or mislaid and is not now to be found but from the well known Settlements & Improvements made by the said Licenced Settlers therein and the many Surveys made round the abovesaid Manor and other proofs and Circumstances it appears that the said Manor is bounded on the East by the River Susquehanna, on the West by a North and South Line West of the late Dwelling plantation of Christian Esther, otherwise called Oyster (to which said Christian one of the said Licences or Grants was given for his Plantation) Northward by a Line nearest East and West Distant about three Miles North of the present Great Road leading from Wrights Ferry through York Town by the said Christian Oysters plantation to Monockasy and Southward by a Line near East and West distant about three Miles South of the Great Road aforesaid And Whereas divers of the said Tracts & Settlements within our said Manor have been surveyed & confirmed by patents to the said Settlers thereof or their Assigns and many of them that have been Surveyed yet remain to be confirmed by patents and the Settlers or Nebelses thereof have applied for such Confirmation agreeable to said Licences or Grants whose request we are willing and desirous to comply with, And we being also desirous that a compleat Draught or Map and return of Survey of our said Manor shall be replaced and remain for their and our use in Your Office & also in our Secretary's Office And Whereas by our Special order and Direction there was in the Month of October in the Year one thousand seven hundred and forty one surveyed and laid out for our use by Thomas Cookson then Deputy Surveyor, A Certain Tract of Land situate on both sides of Codorus Creek within our said Manor of Springetsbury for the Scite of a Town, and whereon our Town of York in our County of York hath been since laid out & Built, But the said Thomas Cookson not having made return of such Survey into your Office the said Tract of Land was by our order & Direction resurveyed in the Month of December 1752 by George Stevenson then Deputy Surveyor of our said County of York and found to contain four hundred and thirty six Acres and an half. These are therefore to authorize & require You to resurvey or cause to be resurveyed for our

The validity of reason (1) in particular is questionable. As is pointed out in Peters' Circuit Court Reports I: 505, in the case Conn et al. *versus* Penn et al., while it appears that a survey was never returned to the land office, the warrant and return were entered in the minutes of the proceedings of the provincial council making the survey quasi legal although the council agreed that it did not have jurisdiction in land affairs. The warrant was dated June 18, 1722, the return dated June 19 & 20, 1722 creating a question about an on site survey. How could the entire 10 miles west, 12 miles north, 8 miles east to Newberry,

Springetsbury Manor Warrant to Resurvey, 1762, page 3

Governor Keith's tract, southeast along Newberry to the Susquehanna, then down the Susquehanna to the beginning been surveyed through unsettled, wooded territory in two days time? The surveyors calculated that the manor contained 75,520 acres and claimed that a plan thereof was annexed to the return. *(PA (CR): 3: 184-85)* Copies of the plan found years later show only general courses and distances indicating that no one in 1722 knew exactly where 10 miles west of the Susquehanna River really was. *(Original Loose survey D-113-125; Bair 86)* By 1752, however, people did know and, when York Town was resurveyed, realized that it lay more than 11 miles west of the river, outside of the manor, ample justification for reasons 3 and 4.

Reasons (2) and (5) were more to the point of the resurvey. In neighboring Cumberland County, beginning in 1760, county commissioners taxed the proprietaries on all land warranted but not patented. Out of 171,315 acres 136,372 acres remained unpatented. After an abatement for 68 lots in the town of Carlisle and 20,000 acres for three out of five years, the Penn family owed £615.11.4 in back taxes for the years 1756-1760. The Governor and land officers expressed fear that the same policy would extend to other counties. *(PA (CR) 8: 472-77)* In particular, Governor Hamilton was concerned about the large number of unpatented tracts in Springetsbury Manor.

Taxation had become a serious issue in Pennsylvania causing great division between the Governor and Assembly. Before the war with the French and their allies the Indians, no attempts had been made to include the proprietary estate in any general land tax bill. When the war began, the Penn family contributed £5,000 as a gift, and the Assembly agreed to exclude their lands from the war time land tax and supply bills of 1755, 1757, and 1758. *(PA (CR) 8: 278-80)* By 1759, Pennsylvania had granted the Crown more than half a million pounds toward the war effort through special land taxes and bills of credit. Each of the supply bills of 1757, 1758, and 1759 were for one hundred thousand pounds.

Pennsylvania was out of money. Even the troops were owed in arrears and the Assembly wanted to reduce their number to one hundred fifty men including officers. *(PA (CR) 8: 425)* To lessen the financial burden, in 1759 and again in 1760 the acts for granting His Majesty 100,000 pounds included taxing the proprietary estates. While the Governor and the Assembly argued over whether the proprietaries' waste and unlocated lands should be excepted *(PSL 6 St.L. 344 Ch. 513)*, plans were underway to survey the manors of Springetsbury and Maske in York County with the idea of selling all the tracts and to collect George Stevenson's surveys and remove him from office.

Other plans were being formed to encourage warrant holders and presumptive settlers alike to patent their land. Years of neglect during the French and Indian War meant that many tracts on both sides of the Susquehanna River had not been surveyed. Some of those tracts were held by legitimate warrant, but a vast number were occupied by presumptive settlers, the polite term for squatters. Just as the war broke out in the Ohio Valley, the Penns had completed another treaty with the Indians to open a broad swath of land west and northwest as far as the charter bounds of the province leaving only a small part of the province to the Indians. Settlers moved in without regard for their safety and despite Indian dissatisfaction. They also held their land tax free. Threat of French hostility soon forced the British government to intercede and in 1758 reduced the size of the area open for settlement setting the western bounds as the Allegheny Mountains. All the newly available land became part of Cumberland County. The land office wanted to know where the squatters were located before opening the office to new warrants. Thomas Penn, himself, was more interested in encouraging settlers to buy their land, that is to pay for it and receive a patent, so the settlers, themselves would become responsible for paying the taxes.

Blunston Tract Deeds of Release

Being law abiding citizens, but still not having legal control of their father's land fourteen years after his death, Michael Springle's children gathered at the court house in York Town on November 15, 1762 to sign deeds of release to brothers Peter and Michael, and to receive in return their portion of the estate. All the surviving girls were married. Present were Peter Sprinkel, Elizabeth and John Strickler, Anna Barbara and Ludwig Treiber, Esther and Jacob Keller, Susannah and Henry Landes, Michael Sprinkel, Anna Margareta and Ludwig Keefer, Christiana and Abraham Keefer, and George Sprinkel. Katrina and Adam Troerbach would appear on November 17. Henry and Eva were under twenty-one so could not participate, but signed their deeds of release and received their portions later. In return for releasing their claim to the western 300 plus acres of the Blunston tract to Peter, each sibling received an equal share of £350, or roughly £38. For releasing their claim to the eastern 200 acres of the Blunston tract to Michael, each sibling received an equal share of £90, or £10. *(York Deeds A-618, A-620)*

To reach these amounts, the children either needed to agree on the value of the property in 1762 or petition the Orphans Court for appraisal. Since no record of an inquest for real estate valuation exists, the children apparently agreed. Thus the value of the 300 plus acres was set at £532 and the 200 acres at £140 and the total 500 plus acres at £672. Without records, however, we have no idea if this is the way the children thought it through or if some other authority was involved.

A year and a half later, on June 11, 1764, Peter added to the western end of his 300 acres by buying 106 acres from neighbor Frederick Remor. Jacob Kyer/Keyer/Geyer held the warrant dated October 28, 1746. *(Warrant Register, Lancaster K-151)* Originally surveyed by Thomas Cookson on 13 April 1747, George Stevenson resurveyed the tract for Felix Miller when Miller bought from Geyer February 8, 1754. The draft of this 1754 survey is important for Sprinkle researchers because it shows Henry Everhart as the adjoiner on Michael Springle's 1746 warrant tract. *(Copied Survey B-4-32)* Thus we have circumstantial evidence that Margaret had remarried by 1754 and where she and her second husband were then living.

Felix Miller vacated the tract before 1763 when the land office assigned the warrant to Frederick Remor. Remor went on to patent the tract immediately. He paid the necessary fees on November 25, 1763. Deputy Surveyor Stevenson returned his 1754 draft to the surveyor general on November 28, 1763. That office wrote the return of survey on December 5, 1763 and the Governor signed a patent dated the same day which was sent to Remor. A copy was entered in patent book AA-5. It is important to note that Peter was buying patented land when he bought the 106 acres from Remor. He paid £340. *(York Deed C-30)*

Michael Springle's youngest son Henry turned twenty-one in 1764. On October 22 Henry released his interest in the 300 acres of the Blunston tract to Peter and received £31.14 in return. The difference between his amount and the £38 received by his older siblings can be explained by Peter already having given him £6.6. Henry was satisfied and brought the deed to John Adlum, a Justice of the Peace, for signing and recording on October 29. *(York Deed B-528)* By December 15 Henry had married Anna Maria/Mary Nunnemaker. The two of them released their interest in the 200 acres of the Blunston tract to Michael and received £17 pounds in return. One explanation of why Henry received more from Michael than his siblings is that he had been working for Michael and the additional £7 pounds was his pay. Another explanation is that Peter and Michael had agreed between them that Michael would make up for what Peter did not want to pay out in cash at the time. Henry and Mary brought the deed in for signing and recording March 15, 1765. *(York Deed C-23)*

More than two years had now gone by and no one had begun the resurvey of Springetsbury Manor. Hamilton was no longer Governor. Indian aggression on the western side of the Allegheny Mountains had subsided after the Battle of Bushy Run. Hotheads who wanted to remove all Indians from the Province had massacred six Conestoga Indians living under protection in Conestoga Manor and fourteen more under protection in the workhouse in Lancaster. John Penn, the new Governor, had just arrived from England and he complained that Indian affairs took all his time. Nevertheless, even while he was in transit, uncle Thomas Penn reminded John to lose no time in investigating York County and suggested that he begin by requiring Mr. Stevenson to return immediately all drafts of land he had surveyed for the proprietaries. *(TPP 8: 2)*

By the end of 1764, frontier Indian leaders agreed to conclude a formal treaty and John Penn's proclamation of peace appeared in the *Pennsylvania Gazette*, December 6, 1764. John Penn had also removed George Stevenson. In January, 1765 uncle Thomas wrote again, encouraging John to "endeavour to find out the vacant Land in the Manor of Springetsbury...." *(TPP 8: 192)* Six months earlier, Thomas Penn had written a long letter to Surveyor General John Lukens telling him to take every legal method to force Stevenson to deliver his surveys, but whether Stevenson delivered the surveys or not, Lukens was to remove Stevenson and do the best he could without the surveys to prepare a draft of Springetsbury Manor showing to whom and where grants had been made. *(TPP 8: 98)* Lukens had produced nothing.

Margaret and Henry Everhart, and the 1746 Warrant Tract

About the same time, Margaret and Henry Eberhard, also spelled Everhart and Eberhart, turned their farm over to Michael's son George and moved into town. George was now twenty-three and responsible enough to take over his deceased father's 1746 warrant tract. He had been living on it with mother Margaret and stepfather Henry Eberhard for several years. On the tenth day of November 1764, most of George's siblings gathered with George Stevenson and John Boyd as witnesses to sign a deed of release to brother George and receive their share of £96, or £12 each. York Deed 5404 notes that the tract was first surveyed about April 1747 at 199 acres 34 perches and although it had not been appraised, the family agreed on the value making a court ordered appraisal unnecessary. Present at the November signing were Peter, Elizabeth and John Strickler, Barbara and Ludwig Triver, Michael and Elizabeth Springle, Margareta and Ludwig Keefer, Christiana Keefer, and Henry and Mary Sprinkle. Peter's wife Hannah did not sign the release until May 17, 1766, and although Adam Troerbaugh and Katrina, his wife, are mentioned as parties to the deed, neither of them were present to sign. Likewise, Esther and Jacob Keller were also not present. *(York Deed F-256)*

The next step was for George to buy his mother's dower right to the estimated 200 acre tract. On March 2, 1765, he paid Margaret and Henry Eberhard £130 and gave them the right to the grain in the ground and to live on the farm until August 1. The deed was recorded on March 2 and a copy entered in the deed book on May 20, 1765. *(York Deed C-33)*

With the money from her dower right, Margaret and Henry Eberhard purchased two lots in Botts Town. Located on the west side of York Town and only four miles east of their farm, Botts Town was a development started by Hermanus Botts. He offered much better terms for lots than York Town, hoping to start a competing community. Buyers could own a 65 by 460 foot tract, bisected by an alley, essentially two lots, for an annual ground rent of seven shillings one pence each. The only requirement was to build within two years a substantial dwelling 20 by 20 feet having a brick or stone chimney. *(Gibson 520-21)* Henry and Margaret's lot was the fifth from York Town on the South side of King Street, an extension of High, now Market. Their deeds were dated August 26, 1765 so they may not have moved from the farm by August 1. *(York Deeds C-69, C-72; Gibson 521)*

Margaret and Henry conducted one more important piece of family business before they settled into their new home in Botts Town. Their goal was to recover at least a portion of Margaret's two youngest children's inheritance. The girls, Mandoline and Mary were alive in 1748 when father Michael died, but deceased by 1762 when their living siblings began to receive reimbursement for releasing their claims to their father's land. While sick and dying, the girls had posed an unusual financial burden for Margaret and Henry. On March 27,

1765 Henry filed a petition with the York County Orphans Court seeking to recover expenses associated with maintaining and bringing up, and in nursing, feeding, and clothing,

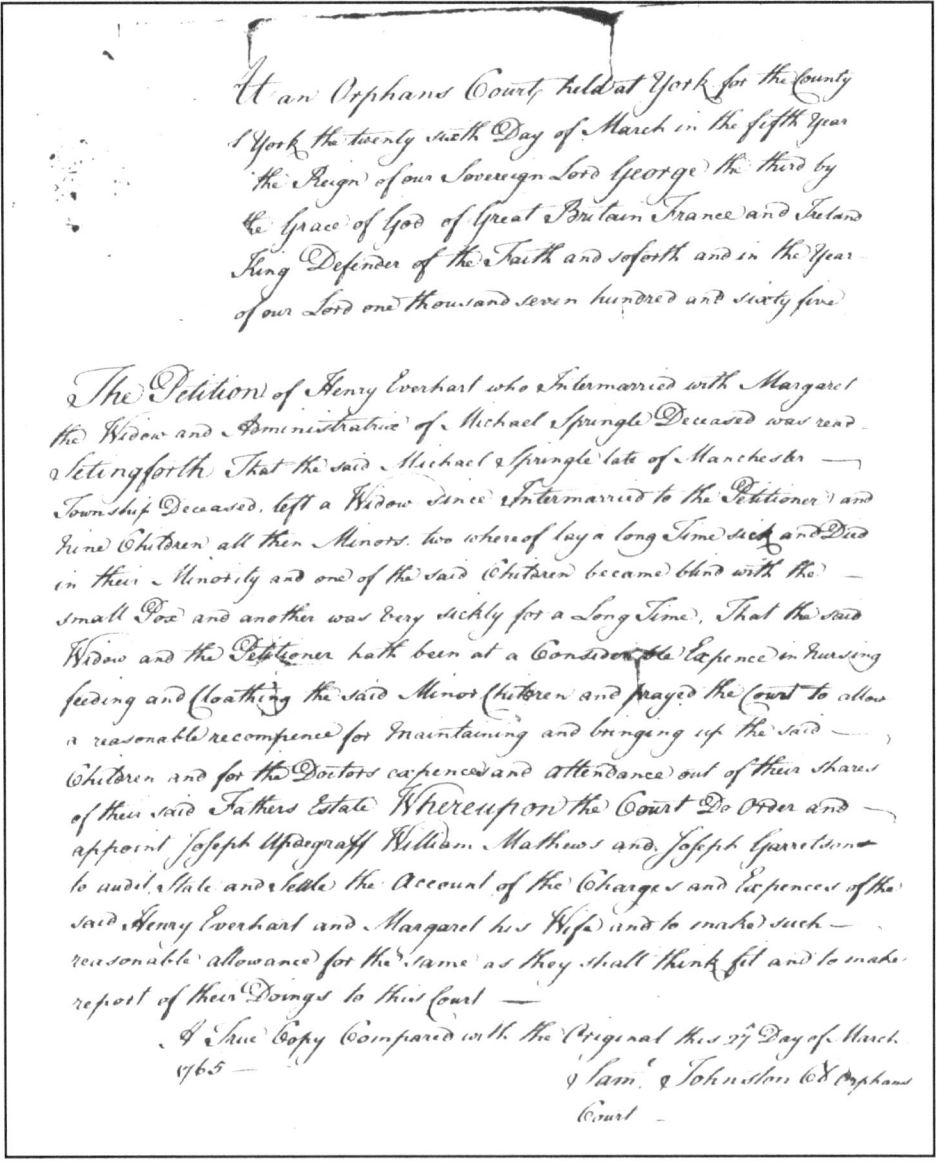

Petition and Order Appointing Auditors to settle the Charges of Henry Everhart & wife
York County Archives

and for the doctors expenses and attendance of Mandoline and Mary. Obligingly, the Judge appointed auditors who returned an opinion that Henry Everhart ought to be allowed four pounds out of the two youngest children's share of the estate. No record indicates when the girls died nor who paid the four pounds. We know only that the girls were in their minority, were sickly for a long time, and one became blind from the smallpox. *(York Orphans Court Records for Henry Everhart)*

We cannot assume from these statements in the Orphans Court records that their father, Michael Springle, died of smallpox and the girls could have been infected at the same time. If that had happened it is doubtful the girls would have been alive in June 1749 when Margaret settled Michael's estate and guardians were assigned to the minor children including

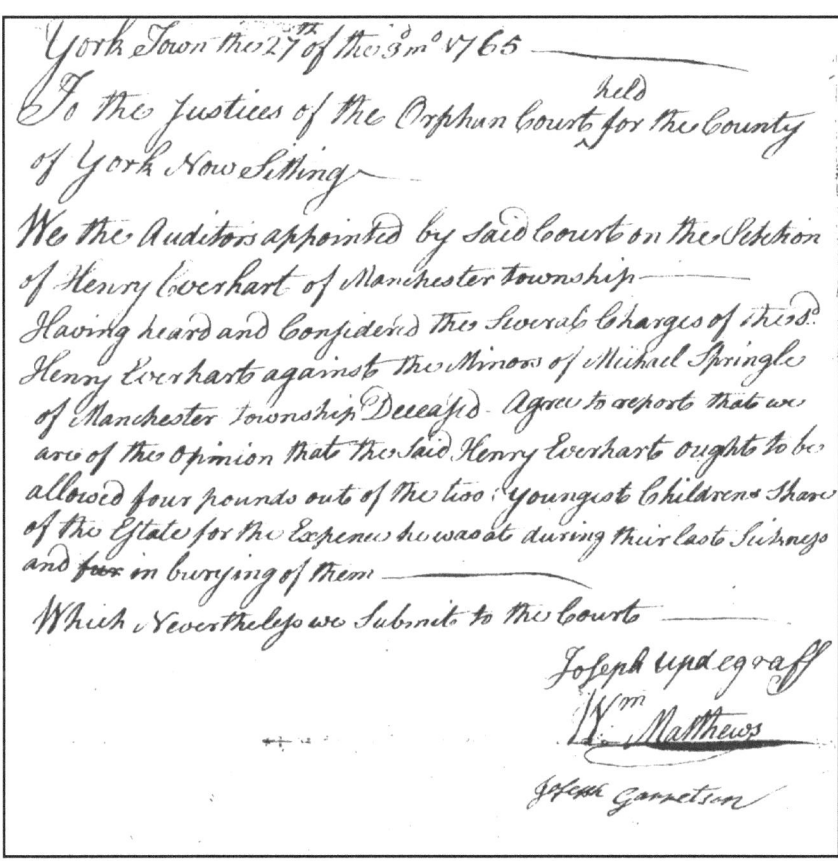

Auditors' Report on the Petition of Henry Everhart
York County Archives

Mandoline and Mary. Furthermore, Margaret was not then married to Henry Everhart since she signed her name, Margaret Springle. We also have not found supporting evidence that the other children suffered from small pox. The first serious small pox epidemic to occur after the girls were born centered in Philadelphia in 1756 where a large number of British troops gathering to fight in the French and Indian War were infected. Another smallpox epidemic occurred in Philadelphia in 1759, the same year that measles was wide spread in the colonies. *(Purvis 174 from Duffy)* Blindness was a common side affect of both diseases.

Eva, or Eve, turned twenty-one in 1766, perhaps in May, or even on May 17 as that was the date she and husband Michael Miller appeared before Samuel Johnston, York County Recorder and submitted for recording three deeds of release, C-133 to brother George, C-135 to brother Peter, and C-137 to brother Michael. In return, from George, Eve received £18, from Peter, £38, and from Michael, £10. Why Eve received £6 more from George than her other siblings is not known, but she received the same amount as the others from Peter and Michael. Eve had been married to Michael Miller for at least four years and lived in Paradise Township. The deed had been rendered before George Holtzinger, witness, and then taken to the Recorder's Office.

Esther and Jacob Keller's deed of release to George for the 1746 warrant tract was dated ten and a half years later, April 29, 1775. In his Sprenkle report, Henry Young, York County historical society historian, mistakenly wrote 1765. Esther and Jacob received £40. Witnesses to that deed were Katrina Springle, using her maiden name because husband Adam Troerbaugh had died in 1770, Henry Miller, and Jacob Mueller. Perhaps Henry and Jacob were Anna Margaret's relatives. Her brothers named on their father's will had those names. No documented genealogy of the Mueller/Miller family has been found and the deed gives no clue to their relationship, but later deeds carry the signature, Henry Miller, Esqr., indicating that he was an attorney. This evidence should also negate the idea that Michael had two spouses, the first named Ann and the second named Margareta. Anna Margaret had apparently died shortly before Esther and Jacob Keller's deed was executed suggesting that they and Katrina had held out to protect their mother's interest. *(York Deeds F-256, F-259)* The £40 perhaps was split £12 to Esther Keller, and £12 each to Henry Miller, and Jacob Mueller as heirs of the deceased children Mandoline and Mary leaving the £4 ordered by the Orphans Court to be paid to Henry Everhart for his and Margaret's care and burial expenses for the two deceased girls. *(York Deed F-259)*

May 1766 marked four years since Governor Hamilton had issued his warrant to resurvey Springetsbury Manor. Still, no surveyors had appeared to carry out the job. One of the main stumbling blocks had been the taxation of the proprietary estate, but that issue had been settled in 1764 when Thomas Penn agreed that it was equitable to tax the proprietaries located, uncultivated land at the same rate as everyone else. *(TPP, 8: 78)* William Peters, secretary of the land office was another stumbling block. He deemed it his sole prerogative to write warrants to survey. He refused to honor the Hamilton warrant to resurvey Springetsbury Manor. Others rumored that Peters was guilty of writing warrants to survey using fictitious names. Thomas Penn eventually realized that William Peters needed to be removed. In June 1764 Penn ordered surveyor general Lukens to conduct no surveys on warrants written by Peters, but another year went by before John Penn removed Peters from office. *(TPP, 8: 95; 329-31)* James Tilghman became secretary of the land office, but he did not think the resurvey of Springetsbury Manor was an urgent issue, either. His first concern was to create order in a system that had outgrown its capacity to function smoothly.

"Fair Hill"

While Tilghman was reorganizing the land office, Peter Springle used the time to pursue a patent for his portion of the Blunston tract. Since the tract had once been surveyed by Thomas Cookson but never returned to the land office, Peter went directly to Charles Lukens, the deputy surveyor for York County and the son of John Lukens, Surveyor General. Peter needed Lukens to do an accurate, on ground resurvey that could be returned to the land office. Lukens wrote on his survey that he resurveyed "according to the old lines as Originally run by Thomas Cookson" but when he completed his calculations he found the entire tract to contain 606 acres 148 perches. Peter's portion came to 405 acres 148 perches and Michael's to 201 acres. Lukens dated the survey May 1, 1767. *(Copied Survey B-5-19)*

Interestingly, Lukens survey found that the line drawn between Peter and Michael's portions of the Blunston tract gave Peter 42 acres more than he had paid Michael for. Perhaps, considering the lay of the land, it made more sense to pay Michael for the 42 acres so Peter and Michael signed and recorded on March 8, 1768, a deed of transfer in which Peter agreed to pay Michael £120 pounds for the 42 acres. *(York Deed C-408)*

On May 13, 1768, Tilghman issued a new warrant to John Lukens, Surveyor General stating "There being a Necesity for resurveying the Manour of Springetsbury as soon as posible .... proceed with all Expedition to run at least the Outlines" as mentioned in the warrant of resurvey dated May 21, 1762. As for running the outlines of all the tracts within the manor, that could be postponed "till a time of more liesure." The warrant ended by requesting the layout of the Town of York and environs if the opportunity allowed. John Lukens immediately sent a copy of the warrant to his son, Charles, who made the resurvey during the last half of June. The new configuration contained 64,520 acres, 11,000 acres less than the original and none of the barren land. *(Copied Survey D-82-247; D-113-180)*

At the same time, Peter Springle agreed to accept Charles Lukens' survey and paid £15.10 per 100 acres for a total of £62.18.2 for his 405 acres 148 perches. The warrant to accept signed by John Penn and the return of survey signed by John Lukens were both dated May 8, 1769. The patent signed by John Penn was dated the next day, May 9, 1769. This was common land office procedure when warrants to accept were involved.

Writing a warrant to accept on a survey that had been done years earlier or long after a presumptive settler had squatted, improved, and cultivated the land became a common procedure beginning in 1765. One of Tilghman's projects in reorganizing the land office was to title all settled, unwarranted land before opening the land office to new sales. He began with the east side of the Susquehanna, then moved on to the west side. From August 1766 to August 1769 the land office received 5,595 applications from west side settlers. *(Munger 77-78; West Side Applications Register)*

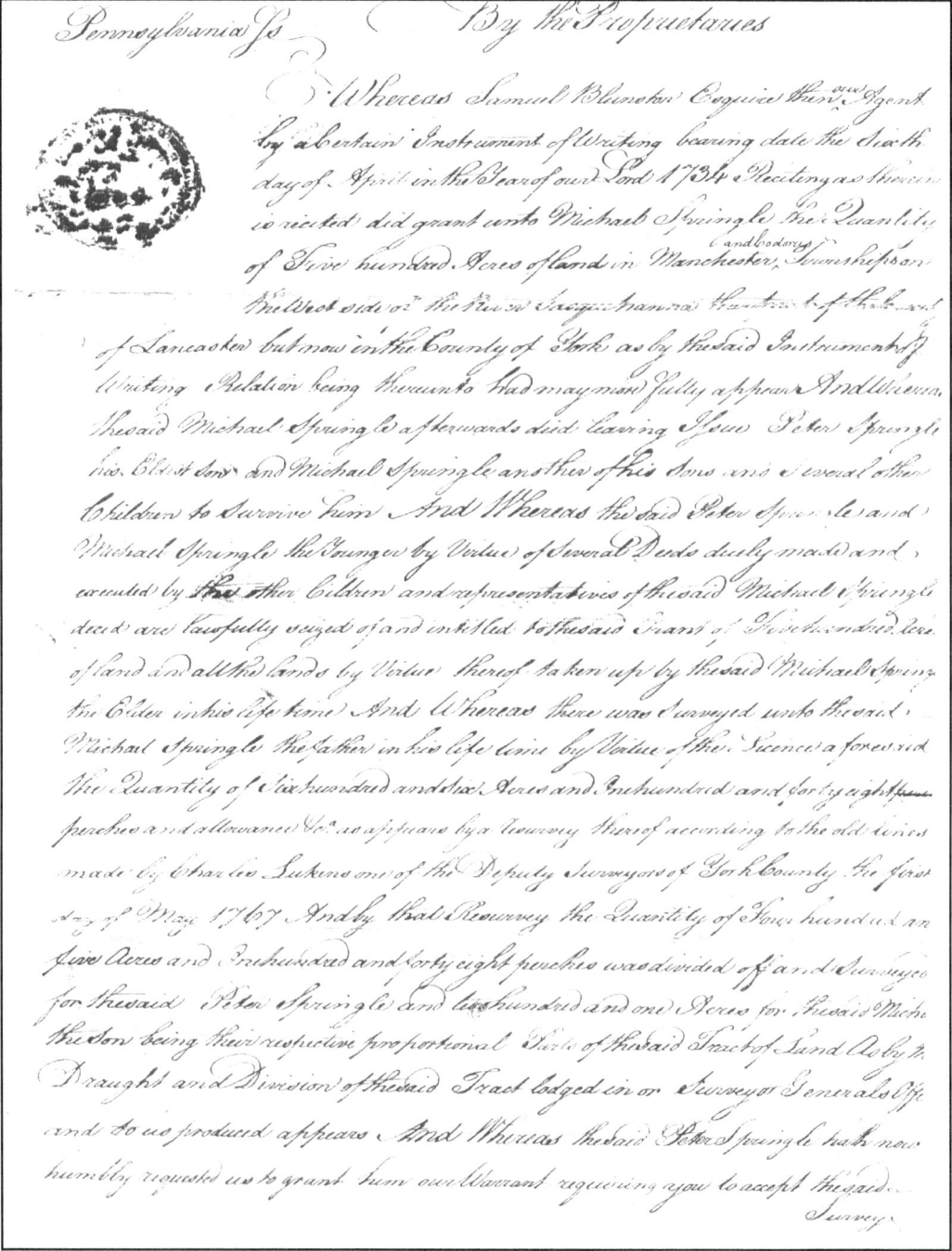

Peter Springle Warrant to Accept
(Continued next page)

Peter Springle Warrant to Accept, con't.
Original Warrants, York S-29, Pennsylvania State Archives

Peter's patent stated, as many others in York County did, that he held his land as of the Manor Maske which required him to pay an annual quitrent of one half penny per acre. Springetsbury Manor was not mentioned in the patent. As was necessary, Peter needed to name his newly patented property; he chose "Fair Hill." *(Warrant Register York S-292; Patent Book AA-11-70)*

Owning a patent or deed that transferred title from the proprietaries to himself gave Peter some degree of security. After his death, and after Pennsylvania statehood, Peter's patent would be used as a test to determine whether the Penn family had a right to that tract as part of Springetsbury Manor or whether the Blunston License held precedence. For 1769 however, it was enough for Peter to pursue his goal of building a saw mill and a hemp mill.

Patent to Peter Springle
Patent Book AA-11-70, Pennsylvania State Archives

Peter Builds His Mills

From Samuel Johnston and Michael Swope, Peter was able to buy 75 acres 121 perches on the east side of Codorus Creek and opposite the 1746 warrant tract. This was one of several vacant pieces of land that originally was outside, but on resurvey lay inside Springetsbury Manor. People like Johnston and Swope, both attorneys and justices of the peace, were warranting vacant tracts when identified, probably for speculation. The Johnston and Swope warrant was dated March 29, 1768 and surveyed December 13, 1771 when they attached the name "Pine Hill" to the tract. The possibility exists that Peter asked Johnston and Swope to act as intermediaries to hold the tract while he completed patenting his own large tract. At any rate, Peter paid Johnston and Swope £30 on December 18, 1771, perhaps thinking of it as potential land for his mills. *(York Deed E-8, Copied Survey A-29-262, Hively, Springetsbury Map S-34)*

George, however, owned the land where Peter wanted to build the mill dam. In 1775 they agreed on the location, a marked maple tree about eighty-three perches (1,369.5 feet) up the creek from the boundary line between their properties. Peter paid George £30 for the right to build. The deed between the brothers laid out very specific requirements. The height or depth of the dam was to be no more than six feet; the race ditch or conduit of twelve feet in breadth and 43 perches (709.5 feet) in length was to be three feet deep. They also agreed to free ingress and egress and that neither would interrupt the other's use of water. The deed was dated March 17, 1775, but was not recorded until October 15, 1826. Judging from Neal Hively's warrant tract map, the deed describes the probable mill location as the meeting point of the Blunston, the 1746 warrant, and the Johnston and Swope warrant tracts. That point would have been 43 perches northeast of Codorus Creek where it ran through George's property. *(York Deed 3I-203)*

Peter built his saw mill first. As the 1781 York County Transcript of Taxables shows, he was assessed double for his saw mill and thirty acres, one horse, and two cattle in Codorus Township, £1.15 in all. *(PA (3): 467)* By 1783 he also had his hemp mill, listed as grist mill, in operation. The list of taxables for that year credited him with the full 75 acres of the Johnston and Swope tract and 9 inhabitants. *(PA (3): 681)* Date built information in the Grant Voaden Mill Collection at the York County Heritage Trust, and online, should be changed to reflect the more exact dates as should also the mill type. As mentioned earlier, grist mills often served as hemp and oil mills which Peter's did, according to the United States Direct Tax of 1798 and York County tax lists discussed later. Both mills were definitely in operation in 1789 when Peter, Jr. filed his petition to partition or value his father's estate. *(Peter Sprenkle Estate, York County Orphans Court May 26, 1789. June 5, 1789, August 27, 178)*

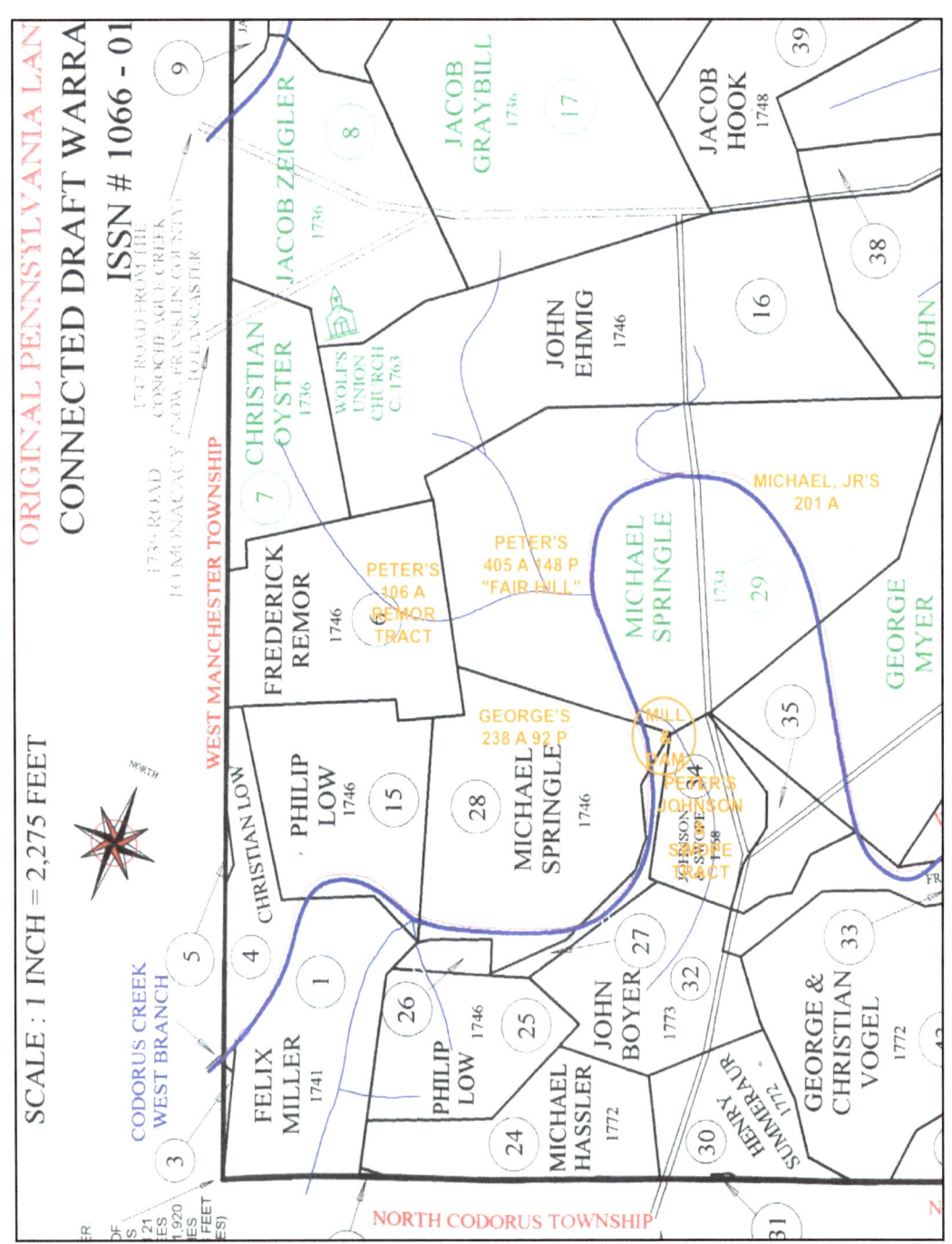

Peter Springle's Mill Dam and other Springle tracts
Springettsbury Manor Map Courtesy Neal Hively

Michael, Jr. Sells

While Peter was adding to the land he had inherited from father Michael Springle, brother Michael, Jr., was selling his. Not enjoying the life of a farmer, Michael, Jr. bought a tavern and fourteen acres three-quarters and thirty perches on the road from York to Carlisle. This was part of a larger tract Nicholas Harmon, Jr. had patented in 1764. Harmon's deed to Michael was dated March 19, 1768, but not recorded. Michael, Jr.'s first tavern license of record was 1771. *(York Court Docket (July) 10: 136)* On November 30, 1772 he sold his portion of the Blunston tract to Christian Krebill of Heidelberg Township for £700. *(York Deed 2H-12)* Krebill owned the property for slightly less than two years before selling to Andreas Hoke. *(York Deed 2Q-475)* Michael, Jr. had no more involvement with Michael, Sr.'s land, but the sale did not end the family's involvement with the 200 acres of the Blunston tract.

The War for Independence; A Son Moves West

Michael, Jr. might have been able to escape the life of a farmer, but he could not escape the War for Independence. In the summer of 1775, before the war began, Pennsylvania had formed the voluntary military organization known as Associators. Michael was a member of Captain Kopenhafer's Company of the York County Battalion under Col. Matthew Dill for 1776. *(PA (6): 2: 610)* His company was composed mainly of German speaking residents of Manchester Township and was not chosen to be part of the Flying Camp nor was it deployed in the Jerseys 1776-1777. Volunteering collapsed that winter and along with it the Associators system. Compulsory enrollment in the militia began in March 1777. All able bodied men ages eighteen through fifty-three were enrolled in companies formed on a geographic basis. Exercise drills were infrequent, but mandatory. Men failing to attend were fined. As a private of the sixth class in Capt. Copenhaeffer's company, Michael did not attend exercises and owed £37.10.0 in fines for the three year period 1777-1780. *(PA (3): 7: 109)* The most that anyone owed for the same period was £40.

Perhaps tiring of life in York County and not wishing to experience active duty in the Pennsylvania Line, Michael, Jr. looked west like his father before him. In September 1779 he sold his tavern and fourteen acres three quarters and thirty perches to Frederick Leonhart of Dover Township. The sale price was a considerably inflated £2550.0.0 current money of Pennsylvania, but since we do not know how much Michael paid for the property in 1768 we cannot calculate how inflated. However, in Pennsylvania in September 1779 it took 24 Revolutionary War currency bills to equal one bill's face value in gold. *(Purvis, Revolutionary America 106 from Newman 359-60)* Michael, Jr. packed his inflated bills in a bag and with his family left York County. His name last appeared on the 1780 tax list for taxes assessed in

1779. His name is not on the reorganized militia rolls for Manchester Township for the period 1780-1783. The Michael/Michel/Michal Sprenckel/Sprengle/Sprenkel names are other family members. Perhaps as early as 1784, but definitely by 1789 Michael, Jr. now Michael, Sr. and his family lived in Jefferson County, Kentucky, on the Ohio River, then called Red Banks, later Henderson, Henderson County, Kentucky. *(Jefferson County Taxpayers of 1789; Starling, 27, 66, 124, 259, 313)*

Michael Springle's three other sons participated in the war effort little more than Michael, Jr. As able bodied men between the ages of eighteen and fifty-three George, and Henry also served their compulsory time in the York County militia. Surprisingly, Peter, who must have been or nearly was fifty-three, also served. According to their service cards filed at the Pennsylvania State Archives, they were all on inactive duty after 1780. Living in Manchester Township on adjoining properties, Peter and George were privates in the 2nd Battalion, 5th Company under Captain Emanuel Herman for the first three years of the war, 1777-1780. Men were assigned to classes within each company for rotation of duty. George was in the 7th class and Peter in the 8th class. No fines were recorded for Peter, but George was assessed a £15 fine for missing exercises during the first three years. *(Revolutionary War Military Records, Pennsylvania State Archives)*

When the militia reorganized in 1780 George became a private in the 3rd Battalion, 1st Company under Captain Richard Bott. Peter would have been over the age of fifty-three in 1780 so was no longer required to belong to the militia and the designation "Jr." ceases for his son Peter. Therefore, the Michael and Peter who served duty associated with the York prisoner of war compound named Camp Security were Peter's sons and the George was their uncle. All three were on the payroll for duty served between August 10 and October 10, 1781. *(PA (6): 2: 631-32)*

Camp Security was built in 1781 to detain the remaining British troops taken prisoner at Saratoga in October 1777 when General Burgoyne surrendered. Five thousand eight hundred troops needed to be housed and most had been moved about several times. By June, 1781 Pennsylvania reluctantly held the last three thousand troops in the Lancaster Barracks and on the town green. Congress then sent the Hessian troops to Reading and the British troops to York.

James Wood, the colonel in charge of the York camp, chose a site between York Town and the Susquehanna River on the original Schultz farm, then occupied by a tenant and owned by a non-juror and absentee landlord. Wood hired at the rate of three and a half shillings in coin per day, local carpenters, and smiths to make axes, spades, picks, and shovels, to help in building camp huts and a stockade. York County Militia members guarded the camp. *(www.campsecurity.com)*

Michael Springle in Pennsylvania   99

Camp Security field with Schultz house and barn in background

Schultz House
*Photos courtesy of June Lloyd
yorkblog.com/universal*

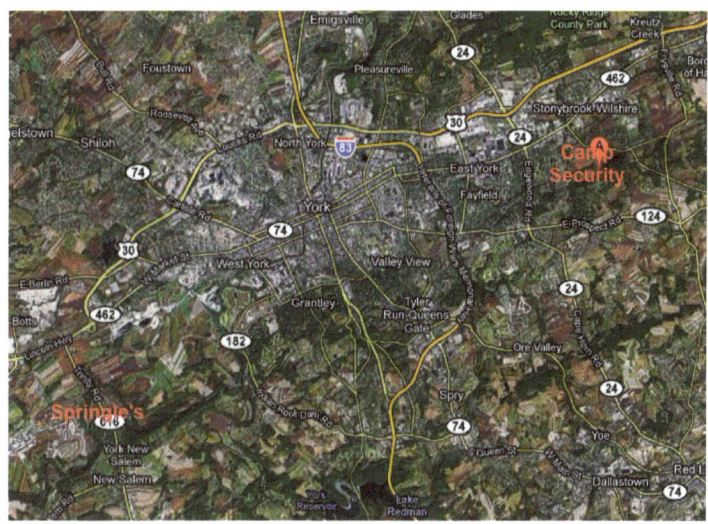

2011 Ariel view Springle's, York City, and Camp Security
Google maps

After the war George was young enough to continue in the militia and belonged to Capt. Herman's company 1783 - 1785. Henry does not appear on a surviving militia list until 1780, but that does not mean he did not serve 1777 - 1780. In 1780, he lived in Germany Township and belonged to the 7th Battalion, 4th Company 8th class under Capt. Martin Wills. Henry was fined £2.10.0 for failure to attend exercises during the period 1780 - 1783 and £2 for failure to secure a substitute sometime during the years 1783-1785. *(PA (3): 7: 91; Young, Sprenkle Reports; Young, York County in the American Revolution 250)*

Although the Springle/Sprenkle brothers were not enthusiastic members of the militia, the War for Independence affected their lives in a very direct way. For them, independence was far from reality; instead of owning their land outright, they suddenly became John Penn's renters. From 1779 when the Divesting Law went into effect, the Penn family was allowed to retain ownership of all their private estates and proprietary manors that had been surveyed and returned to the land office before July 4, 1776. Pennsylvania's new state government would eventually pay the Penn family 130,000 pounds sterling in return for all other land not previously patented. The new state legislature also abolished quitrent. To put it simply, the significance of being included within the resurvey of Springetsbury Manor now hit home. Michael Springle's sons Peter and George, as renters under John Penn, still needed to pay quitrent and that was not the worst of it - manor residents did not know whether their warrants and patents would be recognized. Fortunately for manor residents, while the war continued and for a few years thereafter, the Penn family paid no attention to Springetsbury Manor.

For George, this worked out well. Just as the war was ending in 1783, he became involved as the legally designated care giver for stepfather, Henry Eberhard (Everhart). From the age of nine or ten George had lived with his mother and Eberhard, her second husband, and George had bought the 1746 warrant tract from them when they moved into Botts Town in 1765. Margaret had died in 1774 or 1775 just before the war began and Eberhard had lived alone since then, paid taxes through 1782, and was on the 1783 assessment list. *(PA (3): 21: 18, 189, 502, 684)* He had also been a member of the First Reformed also called Zion Reformed Church in York from before 1754. Rev. Jacob Lischy had been the first pastor. *(Glatfelter 459)* If Henry Eberhard was about the same age as Margaret, he would have been in his early eighties in the fall of 1783 when George agreed to be legally bound to the sum of three hundred pounds to maintain and provide "Victuals Drink Apparel Washing Lodging mending and necessary Fuel" for the rest of Eberhard's natural life. In return, if George and his heirs carried through on their commitment, they were to be the beneficiaries of Eberhard's estate and the bond would be removed. *(York Deed 2C-48)* George went even further and paid Eberhard fifty pounds for his two lots in Botts Town making himself liable for the annual quitrent and giving Eberhard a free dwelling. *(York Deed 2C-146)* Both deeds were dated December 8, 1783, and Eherhard had them recorded on May 15, 1784. To further complete the deal on the Botts Town lots, George on October 21, 1785 paid Jacob Bott, heir of Hermanus Bott, fifteen pounds for back quitrent and a reduced annual quitrent of two pence sterling. *(York Deed 2H-160)*

In 1786 George had his own property resurveyed. He had not done so when buying it from his mother and Henry Eberhard in 1765. What his motive was is impossible to say. His two oldest boys were eighteen and soon to be eighteen so he could have been thinking ahead about how much land he could deed each of them. More than likely, documenting right to acreage along the other side of Codorus Creek was his goal. York survey 5404 noted that the original survey of 1747 calculated 199 acres 34 perches, but the 1786 resurvey added land on the Codorus Township side of the creek to make 238 acres 92 perches giving George control of both sides of Codorus Creek as it ran though his entire property, except for the portion owned by brother Peter. An 1807 resurvey refers to this 1786 survey done by William Kersey, one of two deputy surveyors for York County, on January 14 as the original survey. *(Copied Survey D-62-175)* Still with no word from Penn attorneys about how they were going to handle warranted and patented land within Springetsbury Manor, George did not pursue the patenting process.

Peter, Jr. Takes Over

Following a prolonged period of indecision, the Penn family finally announced in 1789 their intent to sell all land within Springetsbury Manor. Occupants would receive a deed through a Penn agent or attorney if they submitted to a resurvey and paid the full purchase price including back quitrent and interest. Manor residents greeted the news with suspicion of the process and wariness of the legal status of the Penn deeds. Only two tracts in the manor and eight lots in York Town were surveyed and sold. Anthony Butler, the Penn agent, was later accused of misappropriating funds and fled the country in favor of the West Indies. *(Hively, Springettsbury 43; Penn v. Butler 4 U.S. 354)*

In spring of the same year, 1789, Peter Springle, Michael Springle's eldest son, died intestate. Peter was in his mid sixties, his exact age and burial place unknown. That he was Mennonite is probably accurate. Son's George, Daniel, and Peter, Jr. were all buried at Bairs Codorus Mennonite Cemetery. Photos of their tomb stones are online at findagrave.com. Although one researcher has placed a memorial on the findagrave website for unmarked graves in the same cemetery for Peter and wife Hannah, no proof of their burial exists. None of the 139 marked graves date from before 1800 as pointed out by Bill Brick on Internment.net. and corroborated by Peggy Erb of Lancaster Mennonite Historical Society. Further, Hannah died in 1824 when tomb stones were common. The conclusion should be, Peter and Hannah were buried elsewhere.

Peter left his patented tract of 405 acres 148 perches called Fair Hill, his unpatented Johnston and Swope tract of 75 acres 121 perches called Pine Hill, and his patented Remor tract of 106 acres. Peter, Jr., Peter's oldest son was thirty-six and immediately took over. Working with George Eyster, his mother's brother and representative, the two petitioned the court and received letters of administration on May 14, 1789. On the same day Hannah Eyster Sprenckle renounced her right to the administration of her husband's estate. Two days later on May 16 Jacob Smyser and Joseph Grebill [Krebill] inventoried and appraised Peter's personal estate which, with later adjustments, came to £661.2.03/4. Peter's inventory is interesting to compare to his father, Michael's, as they lived on the same land. By the time Peter's estate accounts were administered it was March, 1793. After collecting all money due Peter and paying all of Peter's debts the balance on hand was £127.13.8 3/4. *(Peter Sprenckel/Sprenckle/Sprinkle Estate 1789: Administration Bond, Renunciation, Inventory, Administration Account, York County Archives)*

Handling Peter's real estate had been more urgent. Two weeks after receiving letters of administration, Peter, Jr.'s attorney, Henry Miller, was in Orphans Court on Tuesday, May 26 with Peter, Jr.'s signed petition to divide or value father Peter's land. As required by law the judge ordered the sheriff to appoint, in the presence of all parties, twelve good and lawful men who would act as a jury in an inquest to decide whether the value of the land would be diminished if partitioned, then value the whole. The twelve jurors, all friends and neighbors, met on the premises on Friday, June 5 and decided to value the three tracts as a whole at two thousand one hundred and thirty-seven pounds and ten shillings lawful money of Pennsylvania in gold or silver. Each juror's signature appeared on the Writ of Partition filed with the York County Orphans Court. *(Peter Sprenckel/Sprenckle/Sprinkle Estate 1789: Petition to divide or value, Writ of Partition of Valuation. York County Archives)*

Following intestate law and after costs were deducted, wife Hannah was to receive one-third of £2125.8.0 or £708.9.4. The rest was divided into nine shares, two shares for Peter, Jr., totaling £314.17.5 1/2 and one share each or £157.8.8 3/4 for the other eight children. Hannah's share was to be invested so that her yearly income would be £42.10.1 3/4. At her death the principal of £708.9.4 would be distributed among the children using the same formula as above. The family, however, did not believe that selling the land was an appropriate solution. On August 27, Peter, Jr. appeared in Orphans Court to request permission to buy the combined tracts at their valuation, he retaining his shares and paying his mother and siblings their shares. The judge so agreed and set the date for payments one year to the day ahead. Peter, Jr., thus became the lawful owner of Fair Hill, that is, the patented western three-fifths of his grandfather, Michael Springle's Blunston tract; the unpatented 75 acres 121 perches of the Johnston and Swope tract; and the patented 106 acres of the Remor tract. He also became the sole owner of the saw mill and hemp mill. *(Peter Sprenckel/Sprenckle/Sprinkle Estate 1789: Valuation, Orphans Court Docket 27 August 1789. York County Archives)*

On August 27, Peter, Jr's brothers George age fourteen and Daniel age seventeen also came to court to choose guardians. Daniel chose his uncle George Eyster, his mother's brother and George chose his older brother Michael Sprinkle. *(Peter Sprenckel/Sprenckle/Sprinkle Estate 1789:Orphans Court Order of Guardianship, George Sprinkle, Daniel Sprinkle, 27 August 1789, York County Archives)*

"Fair Hill" Partitioned

By retaining his deceased father's land holdings under his own single ownership, Peter, Jr., was able to keep the mill land for himself and deed other sections to his brothers when they were ready and able to buy. He had no intention of keeping all of Fair Hill for himself and he had found a way for his brothers to pay him rather than he paying them. Apparently the brothers agreed on how to distribute the land among themselves and within a few years each was living on his own tract as is evidenced by tax records and various comments in succeeding deeds.

The family also needed to change how they paid mother Hannah her share. Instead of coming up with £708.9.4 to invest, each son negotiated a bond with their mother, dated from the date of their deed, to pay her an annual amount. The administration account of her estate upon her death in 1824 showed that Peter, Jr., George, and Daniel each still owed her several hundred dollars or a total of $1,528.83. This was one-third of her share of £708.9.4 valued in 1830 dollars at about $5040.00. *(Hannah Sprenkle Estate 1824. York County Archives; MeasuringWorth.com)*

When constables throughout the United States prepared lists describing dwellings, barns, wharfs, and other out buildings in 1798 for the first nationwide direct tax, Peter, Jr.'s dwelling and mill land was in Codorus Township. That meant he lived south of Codorus Creek on the eastern 162 acres of Fair Hill. The tax allotted two acres to dwellings and divided them between those valued at under $100 and those over $100. Barns and other farm buildings were grouped with the remaining land. Tax was based upon a combination of the county assessed value and the total number of panes of glass - each pane was called a light - in all windows, hence the tax became known as the glass tax.

Peter, Jr.'s property contained his father's saw mill, an oil mill, and a hemp mill, and a log barn all on 160 acres valued at $1230. The entry for the dwelling on two acres is difficult to decipher on the 1798 U.S. direct tax, but it appears that the house might have been a 22 x 23 foot, single story wood structure, built over a spring house, common at the time, with only 2 windows containing 12 panes total. The value was $310, too much for a spring house alone. The 1797 York County assessment list shows Peter, Jr. with a log house and barn and likewise places his dwelling in Codorus Township. *(Codorus Assessment List 1794-97)*

Peter, Jr's brother Michael was the first to receive a deed to his portion of Fair Hill, the western 150 acres six perches of the original Blunston tract as shown by comparing the metes and bounds in the deed to the 1767 survey, the return of survey, or the patent. He had probably been living on his tract since his marriage to Elizabeth Hoover. Enumerated on the Manchester Township federal census for 1790 between Peter Sprinkle *[spelled Petter by the census taker]*, his brother, and George Sprinkle, his uncle, Michael's household included one male over 16, himself; one male under 16, son John; and one female, wife Elizabeth Hoover. The only other Michael Sprinkle in Manchester Township in 1790 was his uncle George's son who was not yet a head of household. York County assessment lists for Manchester Township show that Michael was assessed in 1793, 1795, and 1797 and that he had a stone house and barn. *(Manchester Assessment Lists, 1793-95, 1797)* He assumed legal ownership of the tract on March 24, 1796. The deed to Michael from Peter, Jr. reserved for their other brothers, George Sprenckel and Daniel Sprenckel, water rights and the right to amend and repair the mill dam whenever necessary. Michael was forty-one years old. He paid brother Peter, Jr. six hundred twenty-three pounds and fifteen shillings in gold and silver lawful money of Pennsylvania. *(York Deed 20-48)*

Within a year or two after receiving his deed Michael moved his family to Washington County, Maryland where he was enumerated in Upper Antietam Hundred on the 1800 federal census. *(Roll 12, p. 119; York Deed 20-212)* Christian Huber/Hoover and family occupied Michael's Fair Hill property in 1798. Huber's property contained a one story stone house 26 x 24 with five windows and 70 lights on two acres valued at $660.00. On the remaining 148 acres he had a stone barn, 60 x 30, a wood still house, 18 x 16, and a wood stable 15 x 12 together valued at $2518.00. These buildings belonged to Michael before Christian Hoover bought the property. The deed of sale was dated April 30, 1799. Hoover paid one thousand six hundred pounds Pennsylvania money. *(York Deed 20-212)* One more portion of Michael Springle's Blunston tract passed out of the family, or so it seemed.

Soon, however, the Blunston tract began to come back together. Christian Harnish, owner of Michael, Jr.'s eastern portion since 1795 decided to sell and move west. He had a ready buyer in Peter, Jr., who bought the 201 acres, returning the tract to Springle family ownership. While out of the family, the tract had gone through several owners. Two years after Michael, Jr. sold to Christian Krebill/Graybill in 1772, Krebill sold to Andreas Hoke. Hoke later sold to son Frederick Hoke in 1792 and Frederick Hoke sold to Christian Harnish in 1795. The United States Direct Tax of 1798 listed Harnish as owner. Harnish's two story stone house measured 30 x 40 feet and had 20 windows with 300 panes of glass. It was valued at $946.00. His 50 x 25 foot barn on 198 acres was made of wood and valued at $2518.00. Evidence does not show which owner built the stone house or barn. Peter, Jr. was assessed taxes on the property beginning in 1801 and on March 2, 1802 he completed the purchase paying Harnish three thousand pounds for the unpatented land with its buildings. He had plans for the tract. *(York Deeds 2Q-473, 2Q-475; West Manchester Assessment List 1800-1805)*

Next, it was brother Daniel's turn to secure his share of their father, Peter's land, part of the original Blunston tract. Daniel was thirty years old, married, and had two young children, both boys. He had lived on his property since at least 1796 when he was mentioned as an adjoiner in the deed to brother Michael and he appeared for the first time on the Manchester Township assessment list in 1797 assessed for 100 acres, two horses, and three cows. His property had a stone house and barn. *(Manchester Assessmet List 1797)* Dated 3 April 1802, Daniel's deed carefully laid out the metes and bounds of a 123 acre 157 perches tract bounded on the east by Peter, Jr. and on the west by brother George. While most of Daniel's tract was patented land, it included about thirty acres of Johnston and Swope land that was not. Daniel paid Peter, Jr. two thousand one hundred six pounds fifteen shillings. *(York Deed 2Z-145)*

The Penn family made another attempt to deal with settlers in Springetsbury Manor in July 1802. Their new agent, John R. Coates, appeared in York Town without much warning on Tuesday, the 6th. His very presence moved residents to action. Gathering two weeks later, on Tuesday the 20th, they held an organizational meeting to prepare for legal action and called for resolutions expressing their stand on quit or ground rent within the manor and the preparation of a subscription list to raise the necessary money. A freeholders meeting was set for Saturday, August 14. Judging by the future law suit, settlers discussed several other issues. *(Hively, Springettsbury 46-48)*

Coates returned the next spring, March 1803, ready to do business. Not to be deterred by the possibility of a law suit, yet anticipating problems, Penn attorneys had prepared a set of guidelines and instructions for Coates. Settlers who did not hold patents to their land could secure a deed from John and Richard Penn by paying the usual rate of fifteen pounds ten shillings per hundred acres plus interest and quirent from the date of settlement or from the date of resurvey. Each tract was to be resurveyed to determine the exact amount of land involved. Settlers who had paid the proprietary land office any money would need to provide receipts and pay the balance and interest to receive a deed. Coates gave the settlers one week to respond. Apparently no one did.

Peter, Jr., completed the deeds to his brothers in November, 1803. In a deed dated November 19, brother George bought the 106 acre patented Remor tract from Peter, Jr. for four hundred forty pounds fifteen shillings eight pence. This land lay west of and was not part of the original Blunston tract. George was twenty-six, married with one child, a son. He had lived on and/or cared for his property for several years, but was first assessed taxes in 1797. He lived in a log house and had a log barn. *(York Deed 2T-114; Manchester Assessment List)* On the same day, Peter, Jr. also sold George 6 acres 134 perches of Fair Hill bounded by "George Sprenkel Senr," "Michael Sprenkel," and the said "George Sprenkle, junr." Adding the junr to brother George as in this deed appeared on some documents, but later deeds adding George's wife's name, Nancy, identifies George as Peter, Jr's brother. George paid twenty-eight pounds ten pence. *(York Deed 2T-116)*

A few months later, in the spring of 1804, brother George bought back the same western portion of Fair Hill that brother Michael had sold to Christian Huber. George was assessed for the added acreage in 1803. *(West Manchester Assessment List 1800-1805)* The tract lay between George's Remor tract and Daniel's tract and, on resurvey, contained ten acres less than

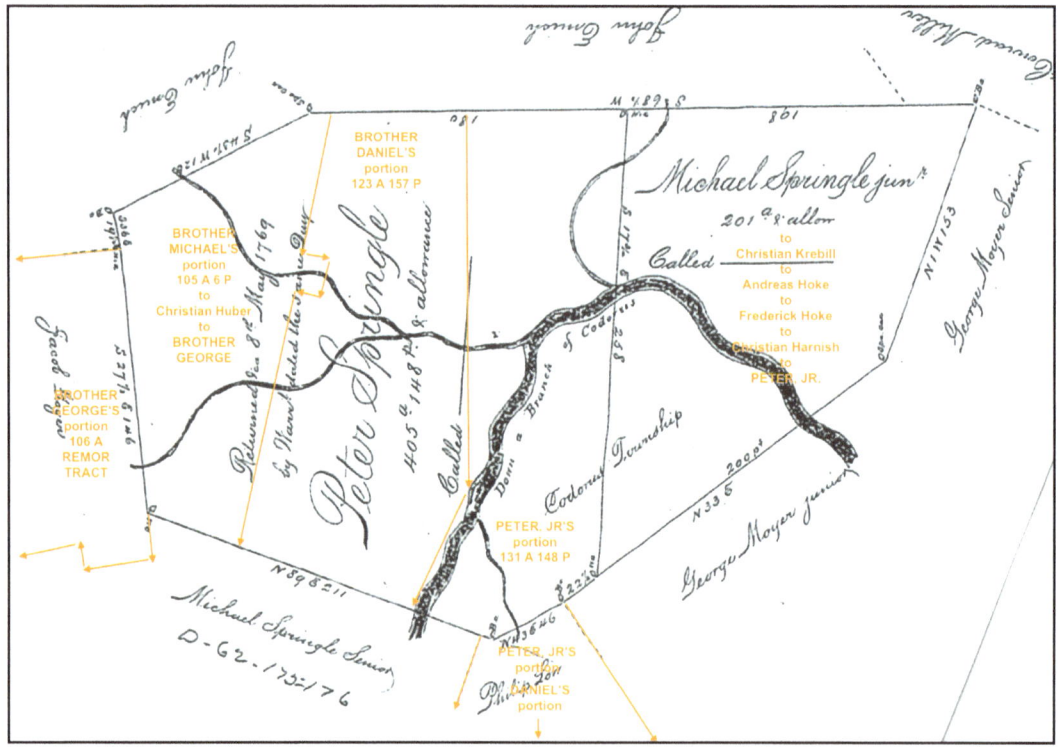

Approximate Partition of Fair Hill among Michael Springle's Grandsons
(Son's of Michael's son Peter)
Overlay on Copied Survey B-5-19

claimed in the transaction between Michael and Huber. On March 2, for five shillings from Christian Huber, Peter, Jr. and Michael signed a deed of release acknowledging the reduction in acreage thus clearing the way for George to complete his purchase on March 8. George paid Christian Huber two thousand eight hundred twenty pounds for the 140 acres 144 perches. The deed repeated the reservation of water rights for Daniel of four days and nights every week beginning every Thursday morning along with the right to amend, clear, and scour the dam and to dig ditches whenever needed. *(York Deed 2T-110, 2T-112)*

To obtain the land arrangement they desired, George junr. and wife Nancy sold to brother Daniel 50 acres of the land he had just bought from Christian Huber. This deed was signed and dated April 2, 1804. Daniel paid George eight hundred sixty-three pounds twelve shillings six pence. *(York Deed 2Z-148)*

Michael Springle's entire Blunston tract was now owned by grandsons Peter, Jr., Daniel, and George, sons of eldest son Peter. The western two-thirds of the tract was patented land; the eastern one-third remained to be patented.

First Court Case: Penns' Lessee versus Klyne

Following Coates disastrous March 1803 peaceful attempt to do business with settlers on unpatented land within Springetsbury Manor, Penn attorneys turned to coercion by starting an ejectment suit against Peter Klyne, a settler. Intended to be the prime legal test of John and Richard Penn's proprietary rights throughout Pennsylvania, the case was sufficiently important to be scheduled in the Third United States Circuit Court, Pennsylvania District, for the October session 1805. In preparation, Coates had gathered from the land office, then located in Lancaster, all warrants, surveys, returns of survey and patents pertaining to residents within the manor. He knew the chain of title and status of each tract. The general question before the Court was whether the tract involved was included in a larger tract called and known as a proprietary manor surveyed and returned to the land office before 4 July 1776. Basing their decision on the existence and results of the 1768 re-survey, judges in the case decided in favor of the Penns. In reaching their conclusion, the judges sidestepped the validity of the "lost" 1722 survey and its decidedly different configuration. Their decision left no doubt that all unpatented land within the resurvey of 1768 belonged to the Penn family and they had every right to sell on their own terms. Back quit-rent with interest on patented land also belonged to the Penns from either the date of settlement, the date of warrant, or the date of survey. Coates calculated the potential amount due the Penns to be about one hundred thousand dollars. All owners of unpatented land within the manor now needed to deal directly with Coates, the Penns's agent. Within a year of the decision, one hundred forty-three Springetsbury Manor residents had paid for their tracts and received deeds from John and Richard Penn through agent Coates. *(Penns' Lessee v. Klyne, 4 U.S. 402; Hively, Springettsbury 48-57)*

The Penns v. Klyne decision directly affected Michael Springle's land. For the first time there was no question but that his Blunston tract, his 1746 warrant tract, his Remor tract, and his Johnston and Swope tract lay within Springetsbury Manor. Peter, Jr., Daniel and George were now at risk for back quitrent on all their tracts. In addition, Peter, Jr. needed to buy anew from the Penn family his recently repurchased eastern 201 acres of the Blunston tract. Peter, Jr. and Daniel also needed to repurchase their Johnston and Swope land from the Penns, critical for the survival of Peter, Jr.'s saw mill and hemp and oil mills. Most perplexing of all, George Senior needed to repurchase his 1746 warrant tract complete with back quitrent and interest from the date of the warrant or run the risk of ejectment. At age sixty-three with a grown family, George Senior had no intention of complying. He had already written his Will telling his executors to sell the 1746 warrant tract, then, as if on cue, he died.

George's grave marker in Saint Paul's Church Cemetery gives his death date as June 27, 1805. *(findagrave.com)* His administrative account shows that the estate paid for the "Tomb Stone." George signed his Will by mark on June 20. Witnesses Peter Sprenckel and Daniel Sprenckel brought the Will to court on July 4, 1805 and affirmed its authenticity, they "conscientiously" being opposed to taking an oath. In his Will, George left wife Barbara the use and benefit of the house with its two acres of meadow, and four acres of upland adjoining David Barr and George Eyster, for the term of her natural life.

In 1798 the house was described as a one story wood dwelling, 33 x 16 having three windows with thirty-six panes. The 1797 Manchester Township assessment list called it a log house. The two acres also contained a wood spring house and a wood smith shop. The total value was $130.00. The property had a second, smaller house valued at $85.00 and a 60 x 20 wood barn. *(United States Direct Tax of 1798, Manchester Assessment List)*

George gave son John the right to remain on the property until the lease John had expired on April 1, 1807. The sale was then to be held, which it was by auction on March 7, 1807. Charles Emigh, the highest bidder, paid two thousand eight hundred pounds for the two hundred thirty-seven acres and three quarters as measured upon a resurvey dated January 14, 1806. The purchase was subject to George's widow Barbara's rights. The deed was finalized on April 7, 1807. *(York Deed 2S-424)* George's estate inventory and administrative accounts, including the sale of his property, are on file in the York County Archives. Among other items George specifically left widow Barbara the ten plate stove in the "Widows Hauf." The final account statement dated April 14, 1807 showed a balance of £3277.5.1 to be distributed among the heirs. *(George Sprenkle Estate, 1805: Will, Inventory, Administration Account, Further Administration Account. York County Archives)*

Emig paid for an official survey which was run December 2-3, 1807 this time measuring 238 acres 92 perches, accepted and filed by the land office on February 12, 1808. *(Copied Survey D-62-175)* Emigh's heirs received a deed from John Penn al. for the property January 29, 1827. *(York Deed 31-290)* The heirs paid an additional fee of $1.50 to the land office January 15, 1829 to complete and close its set of records on the warrant. *(Copied Survey D-62-176)* Michael Springle's 1746 warrant tract thus passed out of the family.

George's sons George, Jr., John, and Frederick moved to Huntingdon County, Pennsylvania where they all became SPRANKLES. *(Sprankle File, Huntingdon County Historical Society)* George, Jr.'s widow, John Sr., and Frederick appeared on the 1812 Morris Township tax list. *(Africa 324)* Perhaps they had been attracted to Morris Township by Christian Harnish who had owned the eastern portion of the Blunston tract from 1795 until he sold to Peter, Jr. in 1802 and moved to Huntingdon County. *(Africa, 323-24)* George's son Michael moved to Rainham Township, Haldimand, Ontario, Canada. George's widow Barbara remained on her six acres, paying a modest tax averaging $0.26 a year 1809-1816 when she must have died as she is not on the list for 1817 or after. *(West Manchester Assessment List 1807-1824)*

For the thirteen years following their uncle George's death Peter, Jr, Daniel, and George farmed and ran the mills as usual. Springle's mill was so well known it was even a named place on the first official York County map. The map project had been conceived by John Melish, geographer and entrepreneur. Obtaining funding from the Pennsylvania legislature, he contracted with deputy surveyors to prepare county maps, all to the same scale, showing roads, post offices, mills, factories, furnaces, forges, houses, churches and other important information. Melish fit the county maps together to form one large state map. *(Melish-Whiteside Maps. Pennsylvania State Archives)* The section of York County showing "Springles M." is on the cover of this book and the first page of this section.

Second Court Case: Conn et al. versus Penn et al.

Peter, Jr., still needed clear title to the eastern 201 acres of the Blunston tract and the Johnston and Swope land near the mills. He thus joined a group of Springetsbury Manor residents who were bringing a suit of equity against John Penn and William Penn, owners of Springetbury Manor's unpatented land. Led by Daniel Conn, the plaintiffs questioned many issues that had not been settled by the 1804 case Penns' Lessee versus Klyne. At issue for Peter, Jr. was whether he was entitled to a conveyance from the Penns based upon his Blunston license and if so under what terms? Apparently, the Penns' had been refusing to convey deeds to persons claiming property under a variety of old titles, perhaps being advised to hold out for more money.

The case was heard in 1818 during the April term of the Third Circuit Court of the United States sitting in Philadelphia. The judges were the Honorable. Bushrod Washington, Associate Justice of the Supreme Court and the Honorable Richard Peters, District Judge. Justice Washington laid out an organized plan for argument that began with determining the boundaries of the manor. Attorneys started by discussing and exhibiting the 1722 survey and the decision to place it in the Council minutes instead of the land office. Next, they brought up Thomas Penn's 1733 commission to Samuel Blunston and used Michael Springle's license for 500 acres as an example. They then closed by justifying the 1762 warrant to resurvey based on the large number of people who had settled on the west side of Susquehanna after the Indian title had been extinguished in 1736. After considering the evidence presented, the Court decided that both surveys represented essentially the same boundaries.

The Court then turned to the second issue, the plaintiffs' claims arranged into six classes. Those claiming under licenses issued by Samuel Blunston composed the first class. Here, again, Michael Springle's land was used as an example. Exhibiting the title of Peter Springle, the attorney restated Michael's Blunston license for 500 acres, his death, the vesting of the tract in sons Peter and Michael, Jr., the resurvey for 606 acres with 405 for Peter and 201 for Michael, Jr., Peter's warrant of acceptance and his paying the purchase money of £15.10 per 100 acres with interest and quitrents from March 1742, and the return confirming the terms and placing title in Peter Springle.

After considering examples of the other five classes, the Court based its opinions on the answers to two questions: are plaintiffs entitled to conveyances, and upon what terms? In Peter's case, the Court stated that since he was the only claimant under his license and his survey had been accepted there was no need to decide whether Blunston licenses extended to the manor lands or not. He was entitled to a conveyance of the legal estate, but was restricted to the quantity of land mentioned in the license and needed to pay the principal sum due with interest and quitrents from the date of the license. This meant that the Blunston license held good for his patented portion, but that he would need to buy the 201 acre eastern portion directly from the Penns on their terms as well as the Johnston and Swope land. Both tracts would need to be resurveyed and valued. Additionally, the Court required that all plaintiffs entitled to conveyances, including Peter, Jr. were to submit abstracts of their existing titles to the auditor who would calculate the amount yet to be paid, if any. This meant that Peter, Jr., Daniel, and George each owners of portions of Fair Hill needed to submit their chains of title. Auditor's calculations showed the brothers needed to pay an additional £86 for which they received a deed of Quit Rents Release dated September 7, 1819. *(Peters Reports 496-527; Washington Reports 430-442; York Deed 3F-214)*

In sidestepping whether Blunston Licenses extended to the manor lands or not the Court left open a question that is still debated among historians. Blunston's carefully worded title to his license book stated simply that it is "A Record of Licenses Granted ...to settle & (0bl) (take?) up land on the west side of Susquehanna River...." However, when surveyors realized that Thomas Penn's licenses "to sundry persons setled within the Manor of Springetsbury" applied to settlers further west than Blunston license holders, they probably suggested the resurvey to Gov. Hamilton. Hence, Blunston license holders were caught within Springetsbury Manor much to their dismay.

Several plaintiffs were genuinely convinced that the court's decree and order in Conn et al. versus Penn was wrong. They appealed to the Supreme Court of the United States where their cause was argued March 16, 1820. The case was heard on the transcript of the record and argued by attorneys Pinkney and Jones for the plaintiffs. Attorney-General William Wirt and attorney John Sergeant represented John and William Penn. Chief Justice Marshall delivered the opinion of the Court. Based primarily upon irregularities in the original case, both that oral testimony had not been introduced into the written record and that defendant William Penn was not present for the statement of the verdict, Marshall reversed the lower court's opinion and remanded the case for rehearing. At the same time, Marshall emphasized that John and William Penn were at liberty to proceed as they wished under their legal title and that was sufficient to prevent the plaintiffs from practicing unnecessary delays. *(Wheaton Reports 424-428)*

At issue in the rehearing, held April term 1824, was one basic issue: to which purchasers did the Penn terms apply? The decision hinged on whether the existence of Springetsbury Manor was well known before the announcement of its resurvey in 1762. To address this issue, the Court presented an extensive reexamination of the survey of 1722 and reversed its opinion stating "we can never feel mortified in correcting a former opinion which we believe to be erroneous." In his statement, Judge Washington declared that Springetsbury Manor was not sufficiently well known before the 1762 warrant to resurvey to have alerted purchasers and settlers to its existence. By way of explanation he said that copying a grant into Blunston's personal license book was not sufficient notice to inform purchasers that the licenses were for grants of land within Springetsbury Manor. Washington noted that not a single witness the Court had deposed for the rehearing had ever heard of the manor either before 1762 or 1768. He pointed out that no evidence of a manor was on file in the land office because the only legitimate source of information about the 1722 survey was in the secretary of state's office. Washington admitted that the 1722 survey, if it had been conducted on the ground, would have named entirely different boundaries than those named in the resurvey of 1768. Furthermore, an attempted reenactment had shown that it was impossible to conduct the 1722 survey in the two days originally claimed. Finally, plaintiffs had shown that no existing tract survey mentioned 1722 survey points. *(Washington, Reports, 430-442)*

The new decision meant that landholders who had acquired titles within the manor prior to 1762, such as Michael Springle, were entitled to the surplus, as well as the quantity stated in their warrants, on paying for the additional acreage on the common terms. That led to the issue of abatement of interest during times of upheaval and war, but the Court clearly stated there was no precedent for that and should not be allowed.

Clear Title

Peter, Jr. and Daniel now began the process of titling their unpatented land. Since the Johnston and Swope tract of 75 acres 121 perches had been warranted in 1768, they clearly needed to deal directly with the Penn attorneys. Each brother bought part of the tract at a little over $5.00 per acre, Daniel 29 acres 25 perches in 1822 paying $149.00 and Peter, Jr. the remaining 54 acres 48 perches in 1827 paying $272.00. *(York Deeds 3G-203, 3I-248)* Titles were from John Penn and William Penn by Thomas Cadwalader, their attorney.

On the same January 30, 1827 day, Peter, Jr. purchased for the second time the unpatented 201 acres of his grandfather Michael Springle's Blunston tract. After resurvey, the tract contained 200.41 acres. The cost was $720.00. Adjusted for inflation, he paid nearly three times what he would have paid if he had been able to patent the land in 1769 when he patented the western portion. *(MeasuringWorth.com; York Deed 3I-247)* Brothers Peter, Jr., Daniel, and George finally held clear title to the entire Blunston tract.

Unfortunately, Michael Springle's grandsons did not have long to savor their accomplishment. During the long, drawn out process, they had grown older. Peter, Jr., was now seventy-four, Daniel was fifty-five, and George was fifty-one. Yet, they had the satisfaction of knowing they had provided for their heirs and they each remained on their respective properties until they, themselves, died.

Michael Springle in Pennsylvania

Lewis Miller drawing of the Codorus Creek Flood of 1817
showing young man saving bottles that broke loose from a brew house.
Ten people died in this deadliest flood on record.
Courtesy yorkblog.com

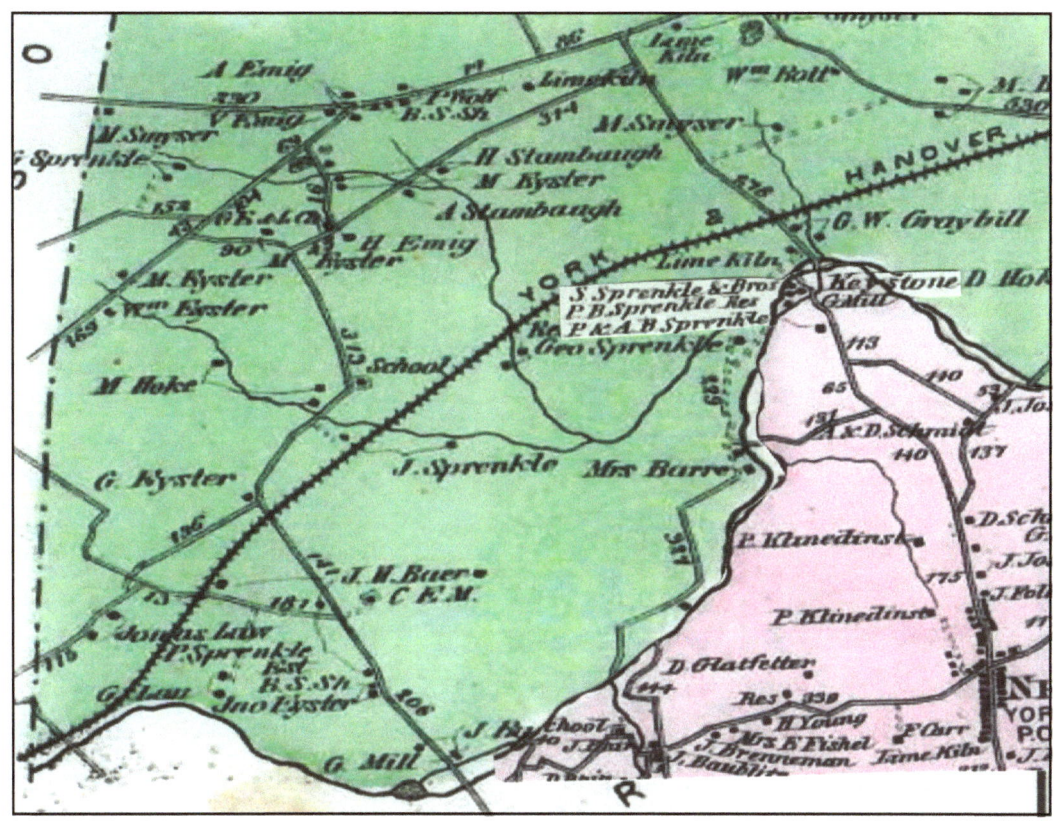

Sprenkle Residences and Businesses, 1876, on and near Michael Springle's Blunston Tract
Composite of West Manchester (green) and North Codorus (pink) Townships
Beach Nichols. Atlas of York Co., Pennsylvania, 1876

4 Epilogue

Michael Springle's Blunston tract remained in the family for several years after grandsons Peter, Jr., Daniel, and George died. Youngest grandson George's property was the first to change ownership. Upon George's death in 1828 an inquest jury merged his western portion of the Blunston tract with his Remor tract adjoining to the west, then partitioned the whole into two tracts, north and south and a third small, woodland tract. Eldest son David relinquished his right and bought a 139 acre nearby farm from Peter Menges, part of the original Jacob Ziegler tract. *(York Deed 3K-223)* Daughter Barbara and husband Joseph Stoner bought the small woodland tract. *(George Sprenkle Estate1828, York County Archives)*

That left the two north and south properties to second son Peter and third son George. Peter selected the southern tract of 97 acres 137 perches, arbitrarily called tract 2, in 1829 when he turned twenty-one. In 1880 Peter and wife Catherine Stoner Sprenkle still lived on their tract; son Samuel S. lived in the next dwelling, son Jacob lived nearby, and deceased son Peter S.'s widow, Matilda and her two living sons, Joseph W. and Hollingsworth, also lived nearby. When George turned twenty-one in 1834 he took the northern tract 1 of 105 acres 57 perches. He outlived two wives and in 1880 still lived on his farm. Grandson Ellsworth Bechtel, age 16, son of deceased daughter Anna, lived with him, at least part of the time. Son Abraham H. lived in the next dwelling. *(George Sprenkle Estate1828, York County Archives; 1880 U.S. Census, PA, York, West Manchester)*

Grandson Peter, Jr.'s property was the next to be transferred to his heirs. Shortly before he died in 1831, Peter, Jr. sold his Blunston tract parcels to two of his children, George and Nancy. The eastern 201 acre portion that had gone to Michael, Jr. he deeded to daughter Nancy and husband Joseph Graybill. *(York Deed 3L-280)* Thereafter, that portion of the Blunston tract became known as Graybill's. Nancy's husband Joseph Graybill died insolvent in 1853 when the tract was partitioned and part was sold. *(Frey 209-11)* Nancy continued to live on a portion of the property with grown children George W., Elizabeth, and Rebecca until she died in 1861.

To son George, Peter, Jr. deeded his 145 acre 148 perches eastern portion of Fair Hill and his 54 acre 84 perches portion of his Johnston and Swope tract, land that contained the mills. Both the deed to George and the deed to Nancy and Joseph Graybill were subject to "certain Articles of Agreement" not mentioned in the deeds *(York Deed 3L-282)*, but had to do with providing for their sister Christina, noted as "idiot" in the North Codorus Township 1860 federal census, and the disposition of whatever money remained after her death. *(Frey 209-11)* When George died in 1857, wife Elizabeth and children retained proportional ownership of the property in North Codorus Township. Their son, David B., operated a grist mill and country store that was raided in 1863 by French's cavalry. Confederate troops stole hundreds of dollars worth of merchandise as well as David's three horses and two tons of hay. His damage claim was one of the larger in York County. *(Mingus Feb. 4, 2009; Pennsylvania Civil War Civilian Damage Claims. York County Heritage Trust)* The property remained in the family well into the 1880's. Elizabeth and Emanuel B. sold right of way to the York and Hanover Railway in 1885 and in 1886 son Peter B. operated a firm manufacturing flint, but by 1900 the property was owned by others. *(York Deed 7J-229; Gibson 2: 49)*

Grandson Daniel, who owned the middle portion of Fair Hill, died in 1849. He and son John had lived together since Daniel's wife and John's mother, Anna Mumma, had died. *(1840 U.S. Census, PA, York, West Manchester)* Although Daniel left no will, he had a verbal agreement with John that he would inherit his Fair Hill farm in West Manchester Township and his Johnston and Swope woodland tract in North Codorus Township, and had advanced him $8000.00 on his inheritance. Daniel also owned several other properties. His son and three daughters engaged in a contentious disagreement over Daniel's properties that dragged on for seven years in the Orphans Court and in the Court of Common Pleas. John finally agreed to settle with his sisters and they between themselves so that in 1857 he held clear title to Daniel's 173 acres 57 perches of Fair Hill, part of Michael Springle's Blunston tract. *(Daniel Sprenkle Estate 1849 York County Archives)* By 1860, John and wife Lydia had moved to York Township living between son John L. and daughter Elisabeth Altinger. His real estate holdings reportedly were worth $46,120.00. *(1860 U.S. Census, York, York, PA: 1012)* Since there are seven ways to compute the relative value in 2010 dollars it is only safe to say that John was a wealthy farmer. *(MeasuringWorth.com)* Son John L. died in 1866 and John, himself, died in 1868, intestate, leaving two children, daughter Elizabeth and son Daniel L. who was living on the Fair Hill - Blunston tract at the time. After the tract was appraised the Orphans Court confirmed it to Daniel L., acting as administrator. Daniel L. sold the 171 acres 54 perches to cousin George Sprenkle who owned the farm to the west. *(York Deed 5C-343)* Daniel L. and family returned to Fulton County, Illinois.

As late as 1880, portions of Michael Springle's land remained in the family. In the Sprenkle or male line, his fourth generation great grandsons Peter and George, sons of grandson George, lived on farms on the western portion of the Blunston tract. His fifth generation great, great grandsons David B. and Peter B. lived on the central portion of the Blunston tract, the portion once owned by grandson Peter, Jr. In the Graybill, or female line, Michael Springle's fifth generation great, great grandson George W. Graybill lived on part of the eastern portion that Peter, Jr. had bought back into the family. If Michael Springle's goal was to provide for his family, he certainly accomplished what he set out to do.

Acknowledgements

Detail is the backbone of this monograph. Dedicated contributions to our bank of knowledge by others have contributed materially. Dr. Neal Otto Hively's gigantic undertaking, Original Pennsylvania Land Records Series for York County and accompanying connected draft survey maps, provided essential information. Neal began his project when I was Chief of the Division of Land Records at the Pennsylvania State Archives preparing to merging the records with the other archival holdings. I had just announced an appeal for volunteers to continue the warrantee tract mapping program when Neal stepped forward. For the rest of the story, see his website. Suffice it to say, Neal's work is basic to York County research. I thank him for saving me research time, for his generosity in answering my questions, and for giving permission to include his Springettsbury Manor map, within.

To Margaret Sprinkle Sopp, who has researched and collected, and is happy to provide, vital statistics data for the greater Sprinkle/Sprenkle/Sprankle family, I also owe considerable gratitude.

Others who kindly assisted me in my quest for records were Jonathan Stayer and Jan Kinzer, Pennsylvania State Archives; Kim Bucklaw and staff, Chester County Archives; Ken Hoak, Conestoga Area Historical Society; and Autumn, intern, Huntingdon County Historical Society. For special assistance in obtaining copies of Rudy Miller's and Michael Sprinkle's original wills, I thank John Bennawit, Lancaster County Archives. I also owe special thanks to Peggy Erb and Steve Ness, Lancaster Mennonite Historical Society; Heather Tennies, Director of Archival Services, LancasterHistory.org; Lila Fourhman-Shaull, Director of Library and Archives, York County Heritage Trust; and Gertm, Books We Own. Finally, my sincere gratitude to York County Archives for operating the best system for obtaining records of any that I have used since the Internet became available.

For editorial assistance and to help make this book more readable for those who are not immersed in the topic, I have relied upon the astute comments and recommendations of Diane and Bruce Hancock who both read their way through the manuscript in an early form. In a more polished form, my daughter, Ailene A. Munger, DMA, set up an editorial workshop in which she, husband, Richard Albrecht, and daughter, Caitlyn MacKay worked their way through the manuscript in assembly line fashion. Their combined assistance has made this a better book and I thank them all.

Last, but certainly not least, I thank my standard poodle, Graphic SilverSpirit, for her patience and for her insistence upon taking breaks.

NOTES AND SOURCES

Abbreviations

AOMOL: Archives of Maryland Online. Web.
CR: Colonial Records Part of the Published Pennsylvania Archives (see following).
PA: Published Pennsylvania Archives. 135 volumes of colonial and state records in ten series numbered CR and 1 through 9. For detail see online: PA State Archives, Research Topics, The Published Pennsylvania Archives. Web.
PSL: Pennsylvania Session Laws. Statutes at Large. Web.
TPP: Thomas Penn Papers

Names

Surnames appear as spelled in the document referenced. Since spelling varied for the same person, an indiviual's name may appear with different spellings.
The original spelling of Springetsbury with a single t is used throughout, instead of the more recent spelling with a double t.
Original settlers called the Conestoga waterway a creek as surveys show, however creek and river are now interchanged.

Manuscript and Records Collections

Archives of Maryland Online. Vol. 39: Proceedings and Acts of the General Assembly, 1733 - 1736; Vol. 28: *Proceedings of the Council of Maryland, 1732 - 1753*. Web.
Atkinson, Stephen Estate Inventory, 1742: Folio 2 A box 1. LancasterHistory.org
Atkinson, Stephen, Will. Book A1-72. Lancaster County Archives.
Blunston Licenses. A Record of Licenses Granted to Sundry Persons to Settle & Take Up Land on the West Side of Susquehanna River. Proprietary Papers, Folder 12. Pennsylvania State Archives, RG 17, Records of the Land Office. Photocopy, Hand Copy, Microfilm. Best online source: Donehoo, George P., *A History of the Cumberland Valley in Pennsylvania*, 1930, I: 39-72. Print. Web.
Chester County Deed Book Index 1688-1820. Chester County Archives. Web.
Chester County Tax Index 1715-1740. Tax Indexes 1715-1799. Chester County Archives. Web.
Chester County Tax Lists: Conestoga Township 1718-19 - 1726-27, Chester County Archives.
Chester County Warrant Register. Pennsylvania State Archives, RG 17, Records of the Land Office. Print. Web. Microfilm.
Codorus Township Assessment Lists 1794-97 FHL Film 1449188
Cope, Gilbert. Collections of Family Data. Collections of the Genealogical Society of Pennsylvania 75. FHLFilm 517065.
Copied Survey Books, 1681-1912. Pennsylvania State Archives. Print. Web.
   Copies of original surveys, redrawn and bound in five series, A, B, BB, C, D (D-91 - D-114 not copied).
Everhart, Henry, 1765, Orphans Court Docket: Petition, Order Appointing Auditors, Auditors' Opinion. York County Archives.

Lancaster County Deed Index. Grantor and Partial Grantee, 1729-1893. Southern Lancaster County Historical Society. Web. Deeds may be online at the Lancaster County Court House website. A link goes directly to the E-Film Reader.

Lancaster County Minute Book and Tax Notes 1729 - 1844. FHL Film 0021448

Lancaster County, "Tax List 1718 - 1726." Cope Collection, Genealogical Society of Pennsylvania. FHL Film 383296.

Lancaster County Warrant Register. Pennsylvania State Archives, RG 17, Records of the Land Office. Print. Web. Microfilm.

Manchester Township Assessment Lists 1793-95 FHL Film 1449187; 1797 FHL Film 1449188

Melish-Whiteside Maps, 1816-1821. Pennsylvania State Archives, RG 17, Records of the Land Office. Web. Print.

Miller, Roudy-Rudey, Will, Original, Loose; Will Book copy: A1-9-10, Item 2. Lancaster County Archives.

Miller, Rudy Estate Inventory, 1732/3: Folio 3 box 79. LancasterHistory.org.

Old Rights Register Bucks and Chester. Pennsylvania State Archives, RG 17, Records of the Land Office. Web. Print. Microfilm

Original Surveys, Loose. Pennsylvania State Archives, RG 17, Records of the Land Office. Print. Microfilm.

Patent Books. Pennsylvania State Archives, RG 17, Records of the Land Office.. Print. Microfilm.

Patent Indexes. Pennsylvania State Archives, RG 17, Records of the Land Office. Print. Web. Microfilm.

Patent Tract Name Index. Pennsylvania State Archives, RG 17, Records of the Land Office. Print. Web. Microfilm.

Pennsylvania Archives. Colonial Records plus Nine Series (1-9) published 1838-1935. 135 Volumes. Editors vary. Cited as *PA (CR or series number): volume: page.* See fold3.com for free access to the complete published Pennsylvania Archives.

Pennsylvania Civil War Civilian Damage Claims. York County Heritage Trust. Web.

Pennsylvania Session Laws. Statutes At Large. Volumes 1 - 18. Legislative Reference Bureau, Commonwealth of Pennsylvania. Web.

Rent Rolls 1683-1776. Pennsylvania State Archives, RG 17, Records of the Land Office. Print. Microfilm.

Returns of Survey (Loose). Pennsylvania State Archives, RG 17, Records of the Land Office. Print. Microfilm. Surveyor general's record certifying property boundaries and full payment sent to the secretary of the land office to use in writing the patent.

Revolutionary War Military Abstract Card File. Pennsylvania State Archives, RG 13. See ARIAS, Pennsylvania's Digital State Archives. Web.

Revolutionary War Military Records. Pennsylvania State Archives, RG 4, Records of the Office of the Comptroller General. See Web, Revolutionary War Pa State Archives.

Road from Susquehannah to Monocacy. Court Docket No. 1, 1729 - 1742: 279. LancasterHistory.org.

Sprankle Family File. Huntingdon County Historical Society

Sprenckel/Sprenckle/Sprinkle, Peter, 1789, Estate File: Renunciation, Inventory, Administration Bond, Administration Account, Orphans Court Petition to divide or value, Orphans Court Guardianship, Writ of Partition, Valuation. York County Archives.

Sprenckel/Sprenkel, George, 1805, Estate File: Will, Inventory, Administration Account, Further Administration Account. York County Archives.

Sprenkle, George, 1828, Estate File: Inventory, Petition, Order, and Valuation of Estate, Draught of Partition. York County Archives.

Sprenkle, Hannah, 1824-5, Estate File: Inventory, Administration Account. York County Archives.

Sprenkle, Peter, 1813, Estate File: Will. York County Archives

Springle, Michael, 1748, Will Fragment, Original, Loose; Will Book copy: A1-154. Lancaster County Archives.

Springle/Sprenkle, Michael 1748-49, Estate File: Administrators Bond, Inventory, Administrators Account. LancasterHistory.org.

Springle, Michael, 1749, Guardians, Orphans Court, 6 June 1749: 53. LancasterHistory.org.

Springle/Sprinkle, Michael, Tavern License 1771 - 1778. Clerk of Courts Quarter Session Dockets (1749-

1876). York County Archives. Web.

Springle/Sprenckel, William, 1772, Estate File: Will, Inventory, Administration Account. York County Archives.

Sprinkle, Daniel (West Manchester Township), 1849, Estate File: Vendue, Inventory, Administration Account, Petition to Partition and Value, Order to Partition Inquisition Valuation, Additional Petitions, Decision. York County Archives.

Thomas Penn Papers at the Historical Society of Pennsylvania, 1728-1832 (TPP). John D. Kilbourne, ed. Wilmington, DE: Scholarly Resources, 1968. Microfilm: 10 rolls. Roll 4: February 12, 1714/15 - December 17, 1734; Roll 8: January 5, 1754 - December 30, 1760.

United States Direct Tax of 1798: Tax Lists for the state of Pennsylvania. Washington: National Archives and Records Administration, 1962. York County v. 381-416, FHL Film 351607

United States Federal Censuses 1790 - 1880 [database on-line]. Provo, UT, USA: Ancestry.com.

Warrant Book, 1700-1715. Pennsylvania State Archives, RG 17, Records of the Land Office. Print. Microfilm.

Warrantee Township Maps. Pennsylvania State Archives, RG 17, Records of the Land Office. Web. Print. Connected drafts of original warrant tracts.

West Manchester Township Assessment Lists 1800-1805, 1807-1824 FHL Film 1449226

West Side Applications Register. Pennsylvania State Archives, RG 17, Records of the Land Office. Print. Web. Microfilm.

York County Deed Books Index 1749 - 1912. York County Archives. Web.

York County Deeds. York County Archives.

York County Original Warrants, Loose. Pennsylvania State Archives, RG 17, Records of the Land Office. Print. Microfilm.

York County Surveys. York County Heritage Trust.

York County Warrant Register. Pennsylvania State Archives. Print. Web. Microfilm.

Young, Henry J. Sprenkle Family Reports. York County Heritage Trust

Young, Henry J. York County, Pennsylvania, in the American Revolution: a Source Book, MS, Black Series. York County Heritage Trust.

Articles

Bair, Robert C., "Biography of the Men Active in Early Developments and Surveys West of Susquehanna River in York County, Pennsylvania." *Annual Report of the Secretary of Internal Affairs of the Commonwealth of Pennsylvania for the Year Ending November 30, 1905*. Harrisburg, Pennsylvania 1906. A 62-67. Print. Web.

Bair, Robert C. "Early Developments and Surveys West of Susquehanna River ...." *Annual Report of the Secretary of Internal Affairs of the Commonwealth of Pennsylvania for the Year Ending November 30, 1905*. Harrisburg, Pennsylvania 1906. A 68-199. Print. Web.

"Colonial American Spinning & Weaving Study Guides." handsonhistoryinc.org. Web, from Gehret, Ellen J. and Alan G. Keyser. *Flax Processing in Pennsylvania from Seed to Fiber.* S.I: Pennsylvania Folklife, 1972. Print.

Cope, Thomas D. and H.W. Robinson. "When the Maryland-Pennsylvania Boundary Survey Changed from a Political and Legal Struggle into a Scientific and Technological Project," *Proceedings of the American Philosophical Society*, 98.6 (1954) 432-41. Print. Web.

"Cresap's War*," Wikipedia, the free encyclopedia.* Web.

Dallas, Alexander James. "Penns's Lessee v. Klyne," *Reports of Cases Ruled and Adjudged in the Several Courts of the United States, and of Pennsylvania: Held at the Seat of the Federal Government* 4: 402 - 410, Philadelphia, Printed for P. Byrne by Fry and Kammerer, 1807. Rpt. 1968. Web.

Doutrich, Paul, "Cresap's War: Expansion and Conflict in the Susquehanna Valley," *Pennsylvania History* 53 (1986): 89-104

Eshleman, H. Frank. "Assessment Lists and Other Manuscript Documents of Lancaster County Prior to 1729." *Papers Read Before the Lancaster County Historical Society* 20.7 (1916): 158. Print. Web.

Eshleman, H. Frank. "Old Conestoga Neighbors, 1715 - 1729." *Historical Papers and Address of the Lancaster County Historical Society* 19.8 (1915): 271-293. Print. Web.

Frey, S.C. ed. "Sprenkle's Estate," *York Legal Record* 1 (1881): 209-11. Print. Web.

"Glover Fulling Mill 1740-1917*," Haddon Heights Historical Society.* Web.

"Jefferson County, Kentucky, Taxpayers of 1789," Print. Web.

Keller, Eli. "Flax Culture and Its Utility," *The Pennsylvania German* 9.6 (1908) 266-273. Web.

Landis, David M. "Awakening and Early Progress of the Pequea Conestoga and Other Susquehanna Valley Settlements." *Papers Read Before the Lancaster County Historical Society* 25.1 (1921): 5-16. Print. Web.

Mingus, Scott. "Rebels raid Sprenkle's mill." Cannonball, York Blog, February 4, 2009. Web.

"Penn v. Butler." 4 U.S. 354 OpenJurist. Web.

"Penns' Lessee v. Klyne," 4 U.S. 402 OpenJurist, etc. Web [entry not always spelled correctly].

"Pennsylvania Weather Records, 1644-1835." *Pennsylvania Magazine History Biography* (PMHB) 15.1 (1891): 109-21. Web.

Peters, Richard, and Bushrod Washington. "Conn et al. vs. Penn et al," *Reports of Cases Argued and Determined in the Circuit Court of the United States, for the Third Circuit: I Containing Cases Determined in the District of New Jersey, from the Year 1803 to 1818: and the District of Pennsylvania, in the Years 1815, 1816, 1817, 1818*. Philadelphia: William Fry (1819): 496 - 527. Print. Web.

"Peter Youngblood of Pennsylvania/Maryland." rootsweb.ancestry.com, n.d. Web.

PippiKneeSocks. "Get Spun," knitty.com 19 (Spring 2007). Web.

Seipt, David. *"*An Immigrant's Letter, 1734*," The Pennsylvania German* 9.8 (1908): 367-70. Web.

Washington, Bushrod. "Conn et al. vs. Penn," *Reports of Cases Determined in the Circuit Court of the United States, For the Third Circuit, Comprising the Districts of Pennsylvania and New Jersey, Commencing at April Term, 1803.* Philadelphia, T. & J.W. Johnson, 1852, 430 - 442. Print. Web.

Weir, Barbara L. et al. "German Qualification for Naturalization in Pennsylvania, 1728," *Pennsylvania Genealogical Magazine* 37. 4 (1992): 367-373.

Wheaton, Henry. "Conn et al. v. Penn," *Reports of Cases Argued and Adjudged in the Supreme Court of the United States.* New York: R. Donaldson (1820) 5: 424-28. Print. Web. see also USSC 18 U.S. 424: CONN et al. v. PENN. charitableplanning.org/document 1370643; openjurist.org.

Wroth, Lawrence C., "The Story of Thomas Cresap, A Maryland Pioneer," *Maryland Historical Magazine* 9.1 (1914): 1-37. Print. Web.

Books

Africa, J. Simpson. *History of Huntingdon and Blair Counties, Pennsylvania.* Philadelphia, PA: Louis H. Everts, 1883. Print. Web.

Bankert, Jan A. *Digges' Choice 1724 - 1800.* Rockport, ME: Picton, 1996, 1999. Print.

Betteridge, Harold T. and Karl Bruel. *The New Cassell's German Dictionary: German-English, English-German.* New York: Funk & Wagnalls, 1958. Print.

Bezanson, Anne, Robert D. Gray, and Miriam Hussey. *Prices in Colonial Pennsylvania.* Philadelphia: University of Pennsylvania Press, 1935. Print.

Chalkley, Thomas, and Israel Pemberton. *The Journal of Thomas Chalkley: To Which Is Annexed, a Collection of His Works.* New-York: Samuel Wood, 1808. Print. Web.

Donehoo, George P. *A History of the Cumberland Valley in Pennsylvania.*1 Harrisburg, 1930, 39-72. Print. Web: Ancestry.com; FHL film 1035735: 4.

Duffy, John. *Epidemics in Colonial America.* Baton Rouge: Louisiana State University Press, 1953. Print.

Egle, William H. *Notes and Queries, Historical and Genealogical: Chiefly Relating to Interior Pennsylvania.* Reprint First and Second Series. Baltimore: Genealogical Pub. Co. 1970. Print. Web: Ancestry.com.

Ellis, Franklin, and Samuel Evans. *History of Lancaster County, Pennsylvania: With Biographical Sketches of Many of Its Pioneers and Prominent Men.* Philadelphia: Everts & Peck, 1883. Print. Web.

Eshleman, H. Frank. *Historic Background and Annals of the Swiss and German Pioneer Settlers of Southeastern Pennsylvania, and of Their Remote Ancestors, from the Middle of the Dark Ages, Down to the Time of the Revolutionary War.* Lancaster Pa, 1917. Print. Web.

Falk, Cynthia G. *Architecture and Artifacts of the Pennsylvania Germans: constructing identity in early America.* University Park, PA: The Pennsylvania State University Press, 2008. Print.

Filby, P. William, ed. *Passenger and Immigration Lists 1538-1900.* Detroit, MI: Gale Research, 1981 Rpt. Gale Research, *Passenger and Immigration Lists Index, 1500s-1900s.* Ancestry.com

Friesen, Steve. *A Modest Mennonite Home.* Intercourse, PA: Good Books, 1990. Print.

Gelber, Ben. *The Pennsylvania Weather Book.* Rutgers University Press, 2002. Print. Web.

Gibson, John, and George R. Prowell. *History of York County, Pennsylvania: From the Earliest Period to the Present Time, Divided into General, Special, Township and Borough Histories, with a Biographical Department Appended.* Chicago: F.A. Battey Pub. Co., 1886. Print. Web.

Glatfelter, Charles H. *Pastors and People, German Lutheran and Reformed Churches in the Pennsylvania Field, 1717-1793. I: Pastors and Congregations.* Breinigsville, Pennsylvania, The Pennsylvania German Society, 1980. Print.

Gleim, Elmer Q. *The History and Families of the Black Rock Church of the Brethren (1738-1988).* York County, PA: The Church, 1986. Print.

Hacker, Werner. *Eighteenth Century Register of Emigrants from Southwest Germany to America and Other Countries.* Apollo, PA: Closson Press 1994 in Passenger and Immigration Lists Index, 1500s-1900s. Ancestry.com

Harris, Alexander. *A Biographical History of Lancaster County.* Lancaster: Elias Barr, 1872. Print. Web.

Hawbaker, Gary T. and Clyde L. Groff. *A New Index Lancaster County, Pennsylvania Before The Federal Census, 4: Index to the 1718-1726 Tax Records of Chester County Relating to Areas Later Part of Lancaster County.* Hershey, PA: Hawbaker, 1985. Print.

Herr, Theodore W. *Genealogical Record of Reverend Hans Herr and His Direct Lineal Descendants.* Lancaster, Pa: s.n., 1908. Print. Web.

Hively, Neal O. *The Manor of Springettsbury, York County, Pennsylvania: It's History and Early Settlers.* Original Pennsylvania Land Records Series 6. N.O. Hively 1993, 2000. Print.

Hively, Neal O. *York, Windsor and Lower Windsor Townships, York County, Pennsylvania.* Original Pennsylvania Land Records Series 9. N.O. Hively 1999. Print.

Humphrey, John T. *Pennsylvania Births York County 1730-1800.* Washington, D.C.: Larjon & Company, 1998. Print.

Jourdan, Elsie Greenup *The Land Records of Prince Georges County, Maryland, 1739-1743.* Heritage Books 2009. Print.

Learned, Marion Dexter. *The Life of Francis Daniel Pastorius.* Philadelphia: William J. Campbell, 1908. Print. Web.

Lemon, James T. *The Best Poor Man's Country: A Geographical Study of Early Southeastern Pennsylvania.* Baltimore: Johns Hopkins Press, 1972. Print

Litchfield, Carter et al. *The Bethlehem Oil Mill, 1745-1934: German Technology in Early Pennsylvania.* Kemblesville, Pa: Olearius Editions, 1984. Print.

Long, Amos. *The Pennsylvania German Family Farm.* Breinigsville, Pa: Pennsylvania German Society, 1972. Print.

Munger, Donna Bingham. *Pennsylvania Land Records, A History and Guide for Research.* Wilmington, DE: Scholarly Resources, 1991. Print.

Nead, Daniel Wunderlich. *The Pennsylvania-German in the Settlement of Maryland.* Lancaster: Pennsylvania German Society, 1914. Rpt Baltimore: Genealogical Publishing Co., 2002. Print. Web.

Newman, Eric P. *The Early Paper Money of America.* Racine, Wis: Whitman Pub. Co. 1967. Print.

Purvis, Thomas L. *Colonial America to 1763.* New York: Facts on File, 1999. Print.

Purvis, Thomas L. *Revolutionary America 1763 To 1800.* New York: Facts of File, 1995. Print.

Rupp, I D. *History of Lancaster County: To Which is Prefixed a Brief Sketch of the Early History of Pennsylvania.* Lancaster, Penn: Gilbert Hills, 1844. Print. Web.

Schantz, F J. F, and Julius F. Sachse. *Domestic Life and Characteristics of the Pennsylvania-German Pioneer: A Narrative and Critical History Prepared at the Request of the Pennsylvania-German Society.* Lancaster, Pa: New Era Printing Co., 1900. Print. Web.

Schiffer, Margaret Berwind. *Survey of Chester County, Pennsylvania Architecture: 17th, 18th, and 19th Centuries.* Exton, Pa: Schiffer Publishing, 1984. Print.

Schmauk, Theodore Emanuel. *A History of The Lutheran Church in Pennsylvania, 1638-1820: From the Original Sources.,* I, Philadelphia: General Council Publication House, 1903. Print. Web..

Schmucker, Beale M., *The Lutheran Church in York, Penn'a.* Gettysburg: J.E. Weible, 1888. Print. Web.

Shepherd, William R. *History of Proprietary Government in Pennsylvania.* New York: Columbia University, 1896. Print. Web.

Stark, Les, comp. *Hempstone Heritage I.* Morgantown, PA: Masthof Press, 2005. Print.

Starling, Edmund L. *History of Henderson County, Kentucky.* Henderson, KY, 1887. Print. Web.

Strassburger, Ralph B. and William J. Hinke. *Pennsylvania German Pioneers: A Publication of the Original Lists of Arrivals in the Port of Philadelphia from 1727 to 1808.* Baltimore: Genealogical Pub. Co., 1966. Print. Web. For all formats see Beine, Joe. Pennsylvania German Pioneers Research Guide 1727-1808. Web.

Tittmann, Otto H. *Report on the Resurvey of the Maryland-Pennsylvania Boundary Part of the Mason and Dixon Line.* Harrisburg: Harrisburg Pub. Co., State printer, 1909. Web.

Treese, Lorett. *The Storm Gathering. The Penn Family and the American Revolution.* University Park: The Pennsylvania State University Press,1992; Mechanicsburg, PA: Stackpole Books, 2002. Print.

United States Department of Agriculture (USDA). *Soil Survey of York County, Pennsylvania,* 2003. Web.

Wenger, Samuel E, Mary L. W. Houser, R M. Keen, and Joanne H. Siegrist. *Pequea Settlement 1710: Self-Guided Tour.* Lancaster, PA: Lancaster Mennonite Historical Society, 2010. Print.

Wentz, Abdel Ross. *The Beginnings of the German Element in York County Pennsylvania.* Lancaster, PA: Pennsylvania German Society, 1916. Print. Web.

Maps

Google Maps. Web.

Nichols, Beach. *Atlas of York Co. Pennsylvania, Illustrated.* Pomeroy, Whitman & Co., 1876. Print. Web.

Hively, Neal Otto. *The Manor of Springettsbury. A Penn Proprietary Manor.* Original Pennsylvania Land Records Series. Connected Draft Warrant Map: 20. Neal Otto Hinely. 1993, 1999. Print.

Hively, Neal Otto. *York Township.* Original Pennsylvania Land Records Series. Connected Draft Warrant Map: 26. Neal Otto Hively, 1999. Print.

Pennsylvania Atlas & Gazetteer. DeLorme Mapping Company, 1990. Print.

Newspapers

Pennsylvania Gazette 1728-1800. Accessible Archives. Web.

Personal Communication

Erb, Peggy. Library, Lancaster Mennonite Historical Society answer to inquiry re Bairs Meeting House Cemetery. Wednesday, July 27, 2011.

Ness, Steve. Library, Lancaster Mennonite Historical Society answer to query re Louck's/Lauck's Mennonite Church. Tuesday, October 5, 2010.

Rooney, Pastor Patrick J., Christ Luthcran Church of York, confirmed that the Church has the original record book of Pastor John Casper Stoever. February 28, 2011

Websites
(Besides those cited with other sources)

Accessible Archives. accessible.com
www.campsecurity.com
    Website maintained by Friends of Camp Security
fellspointstudio.com/video/video.htm
    Videographer Dale Winslet
findagrave.com
Graemepark.org
    Historic site of Governor William Keith's house begun in 1722.
Haddon Heights Historical Society
    Glover Fulling Mill.
MeasuringWorth.com
    Highest quality and most reliable historical data on important economic aggregates.
waymarking.com
    Photos of interesting and unique places on planet Earth
yorkblog.com
    York Daily Record/Sunday News Staff and Community residents blog

Index

Affirmation 16, 37, 108
Anderson's Ferry 41
Anderson, James 8
Anna Margaret (Miller) m. Michael Springle/Sprinkle 8, 9, 16, 19, 23, 30, 37, 50, 57, 59, 60-1, 66-7, 70, 73, 80, 87, 89, 90, 100
Annapolis 31, 35-6
Application 3, 8, 30, 34, 43, 47, 93
Aringal/Arringall 32-3, 35
Assessment list 1, 9-11, 87, 100, 104-07
Assessment rate 40
Associators system 97
Atkinson, Matthew 50, 53-4
Atkinson, Stephen 53-5
Bainbridge 20
Bairs Codorus Mennonite Cemetery, West Manchester 101
Bairs Meeting House Cemetery, Heidelberg 73
Baltimore County 26, 29
Baltimore (Town) 16, 41, 45
Baltimore, Lord 29, 34
Barn 64-5, 103-05, 108
Barr, David 108
Bechtel, Samuel 70, 73
Bechtel, Ellsworth (s. Anna m. Samuel H. Bechtel) (George, George, Peter, Michael) 116
Bible 59, 60, 64
Black Rock 59
Blunston License 24-5, 31, 34, 38, 80, 93, 109-10
Blunston, Samuel 24, 26, 33, 35, 40-1, 79, 109-10
Blunston Tract 23, 34, 42, 44-5, 50, 57, 64, 80, 85-6, 91, 97, 102, 104-5, 107, 109, 112, 115-17
Bott, Richard, Captain 98
Botts, Hermanus 87, 101
Botts Town 87, 100-01
Brethren 59
Brown, Thomas 30
Butler, Anthony 101
Cadwalader, Thomas 112
Camp Security 98-9
Carroll, Charles 29
Carroll County 28
Carter, Richard 5-8, 10-12, 14-17, 25
Chester County 1, 5, 7, 9-11, 20, 34, 65
Chiquesalunga Creek 46
Christ Evangelical Lutheran Church 73
Coates, John R. 1-5, 107
Codorus Creek 23-4, 26-9, 31, 40-2, 47, 50, 59, 66, 73, 95, 101, 103, 113, 115

Codorus Township 42, 95, 101, 103
Commissioners of Property 3
Conestoga Creek 1, 4, 12-15, 19-20, 24, 26, 53-4
Conestoga Indians 86
Conestoga Manor 86
Conestoga Road 26, 53
Conestoga Township 1, 5, 7, 9-13, 16, 19, 23, 26, 37, 41, 57, 60-1
Conestoga Valley 27
Conewago Creek 25-9
Conn et al. 83, 109, 111
Constable 9-11, 40, 103
Cookson, Thomas 41-4, 65, 67, 73, 85, 91
Cressap, Thomas 30-6
Crowle, Christian 33
Cumberland County 84
Daunt, Knowles 30
Digges Choice 25-6, 73
Digges, John 25-6
Dill, Matthew, Col. 97
Divesting Law 100
Donegal 19
Ebert, Frederick 31
Ebert, (Hans) Michael 31, 42
Elliot, Jared 37
Emigh, Charles 108
Evans, Mark 33
Everhart/Everhard/Eberhard/Eberhart Henry 80, 85, 87-90, 100-01
Eyster/Esther/Oyster, Christian 80
Eyster, Hannah m. Peter Sprinkle (Michael) 87, 101-03
Eyster, George 102-03, 108
Fair Hill 91, 93, 102-06, 110, 116-17
First Purchasers 2
Five Nations 24, 33
Flax 37, 50-3, 64
Fleeger, Jacob 47
Franklin, Benjamin 33, 37, 51
French 83, 89
Froschauer, Christopher 60
Fulling mill 50, 53-6
Funk, Hans 3
Germans 2-5, 24, 33-7, 61, 66
Germantown 2, 62
Germany Township 100
Geyer/Kyer/Keyer, Jacob 85
Glasspil, William 30
Glass tax 103

Gordon, Patrick 3, 5
Graybill, George W., son of Nancy Sprinkle Graybill 117
Graybill, Joseph, m. Nancy Sprinkle (Peter, Peter, Michael) 102, 116
Guardian, guardianship 57-8, 70, 89, 103
Hamilton, James 80, 84, 86, 90, 110
Hanover 26-7, 70, 73, 116
Harmon, Jr., Nicholas 97
Harnish, Christian 64, 104-05, 109
Hellam/Hallam Township 39-42
Hemp 37-8, 50-3, 64-5, 93, 95, 102-03, 108
Hempfield 26, 31, 40, 51
Hemp mill 51, 93, 95, 102-03
Henderson County, Kentucky 98
Hendricks, Hylecha 20
Hendricks, James 20. 26-7
Hendricks, James, Jr. 26-7
Hendricks, John 26, 29-32, 35
Hendricks, Tobias 16, 20
Herman, Emanuel, Captain 98, 100
Herr, Abraham 21
Herr, Christian 20-1, 61-5
Herr, Hans 3, 5, 20, 63
Herr House 60-3
Higgenbotham, Charles 34-6
Hoke, Andreas 97, 104
Hoke, Frederick 104
Hoover, Elizabeth, m. Michael, Jr. (Peter, Michael) 104
Huber/Hoover, Christian 64, 104, 106-07
Immigration 2, 3, 32
Indian 8, 19, 20, 26-7, 29, 30, 33, 37-40, 65-6, 84, 86, 89
Jamb stove 60-1
Jefferson County, Kentucky 98
Johnston, Samuel 90, 95, 102, 105, 107, 109-10, 112, 116-17
Jones, Charles 33, 40
Kammer 60, 66-7
Kammerli 62
Keefer, Abraham, m. Christiana Sprinkle (Michael) 85
Keefer, Ludwig m. Anna Margaret Sprinkle (Michael) 85, 87
Keith, William 2, 24, 27, 83
Keller, Jacob, m. Esther Sprinkle (Michael) 85, 87, 90
Kendig/Kindig/Kundig, Martin 3-5
King George II 36
Kinsey, John 36
Kittatinny Mountains 34
Klyne/Kline, Peter 107, 109
Kopenhafer/Copenhaffer, Capt. 97
Krebill/Graybill, Christian 97, 104
Krebill/Grebill, Joseph 102
Kreutz Creek 29, 70
Kuche 61
Lancaster County 4, 5, 10, 11, 16-21, 24, 29-31, 33-5, 39-43, 50-1, 53, 55-7, 62, 65, 67-8, 70
Lancaster Town 20, 41, 53, 67, 70, 98

Landes, Henry, m. Susannah Sprinkle (Michael) 85
Land office 5, 8, 16, 25, 34, 42-3, 83-5, 90-3, 100, 105, 107-09, 111
Leets, Edward 34
Leonhart, Frederick 97
Lischy, Jacob 59, 73, 100
Little Conewago Creek 26, 28
Logan, James 2, 25-6, 31-2
Logan's Ferry 20
Lowe, John 30
Lowe, Joshua 16
Lukens, Charles 75, 79
Lukens, John 86, 90-1
Lutheran, Lutheran Church 41, 59, 70, 73
Maggill, Andrew 30
Manchester Township 40, 50, 79, 97-8, 104-05, 108
Manheim Township 61, 64, 70
Marshall, John, Chief Justice 111
Mary Hope 3
Maryland 2-3, 24-7, 29-36, 40, 59, 64, 66, 104
Maske, Manor of 80, 84, 93
Measles 89
Meilen/Meylin, Martin 5, 20-1
Menges, Peter 115
Mennonite 3, 5, 57, 59-60, 64, 70, 73, 101
Mill dam 53, 95-9, 104
Miller, Anna Margaret m. Michael Springle/Sprinkle/ Sprengel/ Sprenkle 8, 9, 16, 19, 23, 30, 37, 50, 52, 57, 59, 60-1, 66-7, 70, 73, 80, 85, 87, 89, 90, 100
Miller, Felix 85
Miller, Henry, Esqr. 90, 102
Miller, Jacob 7, 16, 90
Miller, Michael, m. Eva Sprinkle (Michael) 57, 90
Miller, Rudall/Rudy/Ruliffe 6, 8, 13, 16-20, 60
Millersville 21
Minshall, Joshua 27, 31, 33
Monocacy River 38
Monocacy Road 39-41, 53, 65
Morris Township, Huntingdon County 109
Munday, Henry 34-5
Myer, George 42, 50, 57, 64, 66-7, 70
Naturalization/naturalized 2, 3, 5, 29, 73, 76
Newberry 24, 27, 83
Nunnemaker, Anna Maria/Mary, m. Henry Sprinkle (Michael) 86
Oath of Allegiance 3, 5, 76
Ogle, Samuel, Governor/Lt. Gov. 30-1, 34-6
Oil Creek 29
Oil mill 65, 95, 103, 108
Onion, Stephen 30
Owings, Robert 26
Palatines 2, 3
Patent 8, 14-7, 25-6, 30, 42-3, 46, 80, 84-6, 91, 93-5, 97, 100-02, 104-05, 107, 109-10, 112
Penn family 25, 84, 100-01, 105, 107
Penn, John (1700-1746, son of William) 8, 29, 34

Penn, John, Governor of Pennsylvania (1729-1795, son of Richard, Sr., William), 86, 91, 100
Penn, John (1760-1834, son of Thomas, William) 105, 108-09, 112
Penn, Richard, Sr. (William) 29, 34
Penn, Richard, Jr. (Richard, Sr., William) 105, 107
Penn, Thomas (William) 24-6, 31, 34, 80, 84, 86, 90, 109-10
Penn, William (First Proprietor of Pennsylvania) 2, 8
Penn, William (Richard, Jr.) 109, 111-12
Pennsboro Township 40-1
Pennsylvania Gazette 11, 33, 36, 87
Pequea 3, 4, 19-20
Peters, Richard 109
Peters, William 90
Philadelphia (City) 8, 20, 26, 35-8, 42-3, 51, 53, 60, 65-6, 89
Philadelphia County 2, 3
Pine Hill 95, 102
Pipe Creek 28-9
Poor Richard's Almanac 51
Postlethwaite, John 16, 20
Preston, Samuel 36
Prince Georges County 25, 29
Privy Council 36, 66
Quitrent 5, 11, 14, 53, 80, 93, 100-1, 107-8, 110
Quakers 2
Rainham Township, Haldimand, Ontario 109
Receiver General 11
Red Banks, Kentucky 98
Reformed Church 41, 59, 70, 73, 100
Remor, Frederick 85-6, 102, 105-7, 115
Rent Rolls 11
Return of survey 5, 8, 14-7, 85, 92, 104
Ross, John 35
Saint Paul's Church Cemetery 58, 108
Sauer, Christopher 60
Saw mill 93, 95, 102-3, 108
Scots-Irish 2
Smallpox 89
Smith, Samuel 33
Smoutes, Edward 33
Smyser, Jacob 102
Spangler, Baltzer 31, 41
Spinning wheel 52-3, 57, 60, 64
Sprenkle, Abraham H. (George, George, Peter, Michael) 116
Sprenkle, Anna (George, George, Peter, Michael) 116
Sprenkle, Barbara, wf. of Joseph Stoner (George, Peter, Michael) 115
Sprenkle, Christina (Peter, Peter, Michael) 116
Sprenkle, Daniel L. (John, Daniel, Peter, Michael) 117
Sprenkle, David (George, Peter, Michael) 115
Sprenkle, David B. (George, Peter, Peter, Michael) 116-17
Sprenkle, Elizabeth Baer, wf. of George (Peter, Peter, Michael) 116

Sprenkle, Emanuel B. (George, Peter, Peter, Michael) 116
Sprenkle/Sprenckel, Sprankel/Sprankle, Frederick (George, Michael) 109
Sprenkle, George (George, Peter, Michael) 104
Sprenkle, George (Peter, Peter, Michael) 116
Sprenkle, Hollingsworth (Peter S., Peter, George, Peter, Michael) 122
Sprenkle, Jacob (Peter, George, Peter, Michael) 116
Sprenkle, John (Daniel, Peter, Michael) 116
Sprenkle/Sprenckel, Sprankel/Sprankle, John (George, Michael) 109
Sprenkle, John L. (John, Daniel, Peter, Michael) 117
Sprenkle, Joseph W. (Peter S., Peter, George, Peter, Michael) 116
Sprenkle/Sprenckel, Sprankel/Sprankle, Michael (George, Michael) 104, 109
Sprenkle, Nancy, wf.. of Joseph Graybill (Peter, Peter, Michael) 116
Sprenkle, Peter (William) 60
Sprenkle, Peter (George, Peter, Michael) 115-17
Sprenkle, Peter B. (George, Peter, Peter, Michael) 116-17
Sprenkle, Samuel S. (Peter, George, Peter, Michael) 116
Springetsbury Manor 24-5, 27, 29-31, 34-5, 38, 40-1, 43, 47-9, 79-84, 86, 90-1, 93, 95, 100-01, 105, 107, 109-11
Springle/Sprinkle, Anna Barbara, m. (1) Adam Hoffman, (2) Ludwig Treiber (Michael) 57-9, 70, 85, 87, 108-09, 115
Springle/Sprinkle, Catharine/Catherine/Katrina, m. Adam Troerbach (Michael) 57-8, 70, 85, 87, 90
Springle/Sprinkle, Christiana/Christina, m. (1) Abraham Keefer, (2) Jacob Welschans (Michael) 57-8, 70, 85, 87
Springle/Sprinkle, Elizabeth, m. John Strickler (Michael) 58-9, 70, 85, 87
Springle/Sprinkle, Esther, m. Jacob Keller (Michael) 58-9, 70, 85, 87, 90
Springle/Sprinkle, Eva/Eve, m, Michael Miller (Michael) 57, 70, 85, 90
Springle/Sprinkle/Sprinkel/Sprenckel, George, m. (1) Christina Eyster, (2) Barbara Miller (Michael) 57-8, 70, 85, 87, 90, 95, 98, 100-1, 108-9
Springle/Sprinkle, Henry, m. Anna Maria Nunnemacher (Michael) 57, 70, 85-6, 98, 100
Springle/Sprinkle, Mandoline (Michael) 57-8, 70, 87-90
Springle/Sprinkle, Mary (Michael) 57-8, 70, 87-90
Springle/Sprinkle, (Anna) Margaret, m. Ludwig Keefer (Michael) 57-8, 70, 85-7
Springle/Sprinkle/Sprengle, Michael m. Anna Margaret Miller 1-3, 5, 7-16, 19, 21, 23-6, 29-34, 36-8, 40-5, 47, 50-3, 55-80, 85-7, 89, 90, 97-8, 100-02, 104, 106-12, 115, 117
    Administrators' Bond 69
    Administrative Accounts 74-5
    Death 66-75
    Guardianship of minor children 70

Inventory 71-3
Will 67-8
Springle/Sprinkle/Sprinkel, Michael, Jr., m. 1) Margaret Eyster, (2) Elizabeth Weigel (Michael) 57-8, 64-5, 70, 73, 80, 85-6, 91, 97-8, 104, 106, 116
Springle/Sprinkle/Sprinkel, Sprenckel, Peter, m. Hannah Eyster (Michael) 44, 50, 57-9, 64-5, 70, 73, 80, 85-7, 90-8, 100-06, 110
Springle/Sprinkle, Susannah, m. Henry Landes (Michael) 58, 70, 85
Springle/Sprinkle, William, m. Catharine Ehrhard 12, 15-6, 43, 46-7
Sprinkle/Sprinkle/Sprenkel/Sprenckel, Daniel, m. Anna Mumma (Peter, Michael) 64-5, 101, 103-10, 112, 115, 117
Sprinkle/Sprinkle/Sprenkel/Sprenckel, George, m. Nancy Sherg (Peter, Michael) 101, 103-07, 109-10, 112, 115, 117
Sprinkle/Sprinkle/Sprenkel/Sprenckel, Michael, m. Elizabeth Hoover (Peter, Michael) 194-06
Sprinkle/Sprinkle/Sprenkel/Sprenckel, Peter, Jr., m. Elizabeth Eyster (Peter, Michael) 64-5, 95, 101-10, 112, 115-17
Stevenson, George 42, 80, 84-7
Stoever, John Casper 59, 70
Stone barn 65, 104
Stone house 20-1, 62-4, 104-5
Stove 60-1, 108
Stowman, Joseph 13-4,
Stowman, Joseph Junior 14-5
Strickler, John, M. Elizabeth Sprinkle (Michael) 85, 87
Stube 60
Swiss 2-5, 60
Swope, George 59
Swope, Michael 95, 102, 105, 107, 109-10, 112, 116-17
Survey 8
Susquehanna River 2, 11, 15, 17-8, 21-5, 27-8, 30-1, 33-7, 52-3, 55, 70-1, 74, 86, 95-6,
Syng, Philip 30
Tanner, Michael 33, 35, 57, 66-7, 70, 73
Tax lists 8-11, 16, 19, 95, 97, 109
Tax rate 10, 57
Taylor, John 43
Taylor, Samuel 39
Tilghman, James 90, 91
Treiber/Triver, Ludwig, m. Anna Barbara Sprinkle (Michael) 85, 87
Troerbach, Adam, m. Catharine Sprinkle (Michael) 85, 87, 90
Under Purchasers 2
United States Direct Tax 1798 64-6, 94, 103-04, 108
United States Supreme Court 109, 111
Upper Antietam Hundred 104
Wallick/Woolrich, Michael 66-7
War for Independence 97-100
Warrant (land) 8, *passim*
Warrantee/Warrant Tract map 4, 12-3, 26, 47-9, 95
Washington, Bushrod 109, 111
Washington County, Maryland 104
Welsh 2
West Lampeter Township 4
West Side Applications 47, 93
Wilkins, John 33
Wilkins, Robert 6, 8
Window 33, 64, 103-04, 108
Winters 65
Wolf's Church Cemetery 58
Wright, James 51
Wright, John 25, 31-3, 39
Wright's Ferry 38-9, 41, 53
York County militia 97-8, 100
York Town 16, 41-2, 45, 47, 66, 80, 83, 85, 87, 98, 101, 105,
York Township 16, 47, 117
Youngblood/Jungbluth, Peter 23-6, 28-30, 34, 37, 42

www.ingramcontent.com/pod-product-compliance
Lightning Source LLC
Chambersburg PA
CBHW041549220426
43666CB00002B/17